Speaking Church

Speaking Church

A New Vision for the Sub/Urban Congregation

I. ROSS BARTLETT

WIPF & STOCK · Eugene, Oregon

SPEAKING CHURCH
A New Vision for the Sub/Urban Congregation

Copyright © 2018 I. Ross Bartlett. All rights reserved. Except for brief quotations in critical publications or reviews, no part of this book may be reproduced in any manner without prior written permission from the publisher. Write: Permissions, Wipf and Stock Publishers, 199 W. 8th Ave., Suite 3, Eugene, OR 97401.

Wipf & Stock
An Imprint of Wipf and Stock Publishers
199 W. 8th Ave., Suite 3
Eugene, OR 97401

www.wipfandstock.com

PAPERBACK ISBN: 978-1-5326-5629-3
HARDCOVER ISBN: 978-1-5326-5630-9
EBOOK ISBN: 978-1-5326-5631-6

Manufactured in the U.S.A.   12/18/18

Contents

Preface | vii

Introduction: A New Vision | 1
Chapter 1: The Situation | 8
Chapter 2: Hymn and Biblical Metaphors for the Church | 18
    Table 1: Metaphor Responses | 21
    Diagnostic Tool: Testing Dominant Images for Church | 26

Chapter 3: The Challenge of Self-Understanding | 43
    3.1 Secularization and the City | 43
    3.2 Contextual Theology | 51

Chapter 4: Faith in the City | 59
    4.1 Biblical and Theological Views | 59
        Table 2: Structures in First-Century Rome | 62
    4.1.1 The City in the Old Testament | 62
    4.1.2 Case Studies | 67
        Study 1: Ephesus | 70
        Study 2: Smyrna | 73
        Study 3: Pergamum | 76
        Study 4: Thyatira | 82
        Study 5: Sardis | 86
        Study 6: Philadelphia | 90
        Study 7: Laodicea | 92
    4.2 Gathering in the City | 99
        Table 3: Biblical Images and Contemporary Parallels | 106

Chapter 5: Speaking Church: A New Vision for the Sub/Urban Congregation | 110

Bibliography | 123

Preface

MINISTRY IN AN INCREASINGLY urbanizing context is exciting, demanding, messy, and filled with constant challenges and reward. I am profoundly grateful to those who I have worked alongside of in the process.

Thanks are due to the following who gave specific permission for the gathering of materials originally published elsewhere:

To Nancy Elizabeth Hardy and United Church Publishing House to quote from her wonderful book *"Worship in the City: Prayers and Songs for Urban Settings,"* The United Church of Canada, The United Church Publishing House, 2015

"Creating God, You give us wonderful cities of many people of ages and stages, . . . "

"Creating God, we give you thanks for this quilt we call the city, with its many coloured and textured squares . . . "

"Guide us, O God, Amidst the commercial canyons and the insistent crowds walking . . . "

"Maker – Spirit –Son, God of grace and love, we call you by many names – Elohim, Yahweh, Seigneur, Creator,. . ."

To Joan Wyatt for permission to quote from *Worship in the City*, her prayer:

"Holy God, Creator of all that lives and breathes, comforting God who cares for us . . . " originally printed as *Lament for Ash Wednesday*.

To Glenys Huws, for permission to quote from *Worship in the City*, her prayer:

Preface

"Constant One, in our society we are so used to the convenience of the disposable, throwaway items, . . ."

To Marilyn Allan and David Allan to quote the late David Allan's prayer:

"God of our streets and cities, who sets for us agendas that we would not choose, . . ." originally published in *Crosswalks: Prayers from a City Church*" by David R. Allan, The United Church of Canada, The United Church Publishing House, 1993, page 155.

Scripture quotations are from New Revised Standard Version Bible, copyright © 1989 National Council of the Churches of Christ in the United States of America. Used by permission. All rights reserved.

Thanks are also due to Knox United Church, Lower Sackville, Nova Scotia for agreeing to a sabbatical during which most of the writing took place; to the Collegeville Ecumenical Institute, Collegeville, Minnesota for a wonderfully rich and rewarding space in which to reflect and write, and the Board of Governors, Pine Hill Divinity Hall, Halifax, Nova Scotia, for generous financial support.

The finished product benefitted immensely from reading and suggestions from several people. Copy-editing was done by Erin Labrie. Tracey Miller, my administrative assistant during my time at Knox, worked to keep me on track. My colleagues at Atlantic School of Theology are valued companions on the road of learning.

Special thanks always to Heather, who is my companion and fellow-pilgrim on this always-interesting journey.

Halifax, NS
Pentecost 2018

Introduction

A New Vision

Creating God,
You give us wonderful cities of
many people of ages and stages,
many colours and cultures
many bodies of varying abilities.
thank you for the rainbows, the mosaics, the prisms in which
we experience your world.
Grant us the ability to discern
the hopes and yearnings of the young,
the loneliness or contentment of the solitary,
the busy, frantic pace of young parents,
children, teens, the young—middle-aged—old adults living,
playing, working.
For you welcome us, you cherish us, you continue to work on
us and with us.
Thank you![1]

"Sticks and stones may break my bones, but names will never hurt me." My mother taught me that rhyme. It was meant to help me deal with schoolyard bullies and the cruelties of children to one another. I'm sure she meant well, but she was wrong. Language

---

1. Hardy, *Worship in the City*, 56.

is an incredibly powerful tool. Using it, we name reality around us. Some suggest that we even *create* reality through naming what we see and experience. The power of language is shown through the bible in the opening verses of Genesis where, first, God speaks creation into being,[2] and then Adam's authority over the other creatures is demonstrated by his power to name them (Gen 2:19). In the Acts of the Apostles, Peter and James cure a lame man "in the name of Jesus" (Acts 3:6). Throughout much of history, it was considered important to guard one's (true) name because knowing your name gave power over you. Today, when most people no longer believe in name magic, we still recognize that a letter sent to a specific person has more chance of achieving our purpose than something dispatched "To Whom it May Concern."

Language is a constantly shifting and evolving wonder. The publishers of the *Oxford Dictionary* have a clearly defined protocol for adding new words to that authoritative source.[3] Most of us who use the English language regularly rarely think about the relationship between what we see and what we say. We may even imagine that language is relatively neutral, simply a tool to express reality "out there." We might suppose that, if everyone used language "properly" there would be no confusion in understanding in the world. The truth is, despite the number of conflicts that find their roots in miscommunication, it's not merely about understanding and sharing meanings.

For one thing, words may mean different things in different places and different settings.[4] We've all encountered jargon: when specialized language used for clarity in a particular area of life or work confuses the outsider (whether deliberately or not). With

---

2. In many other great foundational mythic stories, the god or gods create the earth out of something else. In the first of Israel's foundation myths recorded in Genesis, God creates from nothing by speech.

3. http://www.askoxford.com/worldofwords/newwords/newwordsdict/?view=uk.

4. I encountered this rather embarrassingly during a preaching experience in Australia. In referring to encouraging someone I spoke of "rooting for them," which, I later discovered, had a vulgar connotation never imagined in Canada!

jargon, however, we begin to move into more insidious characteristics of language—power and control. Language—particularly naming and categorizing other individuals or groups—is very potent. It affects our perceptions of others. Suppose I tell you that there's a busker performing outside the restaurant.[5] Your response might differ if I say, "There's some scruffy guy with a guitar out there." Those who live at or near the bottom of our society's economic scale are often the victims of labeling by others, as are those with easily discernible physical and psychological challenges. "Who gets to name reality?" is an important question in everyday life.

Consider a simple example: what is the difference between a "terrorist" and a "freedom fighter"? Is it just that one supports a cause of which we approve and the other doesn't? And, who is the "we" that approves the cause? Language is extremely powerful. Martin Heidegger captures this power when he writes: "Language is the house of being."[6] In other words, as some students of language insist, far more than being simply a tool that we employ, language affects what we see and imagine. Put bluntly, if we haven't got a word for it, we may not even see it. For instance, there are multiple Inuit words for "snow." An Inuit-speaker genuinely *sees* more variation in frozen water crystals than I do, limited as I am to English.

This is a study of how we think and talk about—and subsequently live out—sub/urban ministry. It's about the life and work of downtown and suburban congregations. Throughout, we'll be drawing a distinction between sub/urban *ministry* and urban *mission*. The distinction is important because there are a lot more sub/urban ministries than urban missions. Both are crucial. For our purposes, urban missions focus directly on the day-to-day, hands-on, justice-making, and shalom-seeking work with some of the most visibly marginalized and excluded in the city. That's their

---

5. A busker is a street artist, musical or otherwise, who performs in public venues for whatever reward the public offers. For many, it is a financial necessity, but for a minority busking is an artistic or political statement.

6. McFague, *Metaphorical Theology*, 8.

special call and unique *charism*. I confess an incredible awe for my colleagues in urban mission: I couldn't do what they do, week in and week out. There are numerous books about urban mission. You'll find some of the best ones listed in the bibliography.

Sub/urban ministry is different. It may—probably must—include a mission component. But a sub/urban ministry is one located in a city (center or periphery), regardless of its program and outreach activities. As we'll see, one of the challenges to the sub/urban congregation is that while its context has changed, it may not have dealt with that change. Unlike an urban mission that begins each day with a clear calling and some explicit biblical warrants, the sub/urban ministry is often unsure about its calling and searches longingly for positive examples in either scripture or tradition. What is the role of the sub/urban ministry in the twenty-first century?

Do we truly need another book on ministry in the new millennium? After all, it has become sort of a cottage industry of books, magazines, seminars, and conferences: all geared to helping local congregations and clergy deal with the new reality. Some of that material is directed toward the formerly mainline congregation and much of it is helpful. I presume to offer this contribution for a couple of reasons. First, very little in that wealth of material addresses the sub/urban ministry and it is different. Second, I'm not an expert or a guru; I'm a sub/urban pastor who has worked with congregations that have taken steps toward refashioning themselves for faithful ministry where we still have lots of questions. Third, I bring to the task some thirty-five years of serving congregations in different capacities, in different contexts and in different countries. Fourth, the examples and ideas shared here not only grow out of that practice but seek to affirm the best of mainline Protestant traditions. My academic training put a lot of emphasis on history, so I know about our traditions. In the rush to change (and I believe with all my heart that God is calling us to change), there is a great risk that everything will be discarded and the very resources that might help to shape ministry in this new time will be thrown away.

A New Vision

I invite you to join me as we consider several factors that impact on the well-being of the sub/urban ministry:

1. We need to look at language and the words we have traditionally employed to speak of the church, ministry and the city. We'll find that, even as we begin to talk about it, the city church encounters some formidable difficulties.

2. We need to think hard about the city as a subject for our theological and biblical traditions. What can we discover or recover that will aid our efforts?

3. We need to think honestly about the context of sub/urban churches. I want to suggest that they suffer from an institutional expression of cognitive disorder.

4. Together we will look at the tools with which your congregation might build its own theology of sub/urban ministry. One of the realities we will encounter is that all living Christian faith today is inevitably contextual. That means that, even if I wanted you to, you couldn't give us a theology for our context any more than I can give you one for yours.

Why am I so hung up on language? One of my experiences as the primary preacher in congregations has been a frustration in attempting to relate scripture and tradition to our lives in our context. That led me to the consideration of metaphors that are central to this study. Most simply, a metaphor is a figure of speech that arrests our attention by putting together two items we would not normally connect. So, for instance, "burning ambition," or "the long arm of the law," and "arm of a chair," are all metaphors. Ambition is an emotion, an intangible drive that can't be placed in a fire; the law is a series of written statements that has no appendages; and, similarly the "arms" of a chair are remarkably different from those of a person. However, when those metaphors are employed, most people who understand English will grasp the speaker's intent. It's worth noting (and we'll return to this) that as metaphors lose their ability to startle our attention, they are absorbed into ordinary language. We hardly notice that "arm of a chair" is a metaphor because the "arm" side of the image has been absorbed by "chair."

Metaphors are terribly important in the bible. Jesus' parables, for instance, are largely extended metaphors. The images used for God and the reign of God are metaphorical because they are not literally descriptive. However, any list of names for God from the bible will contain some items that shock us. [7] While "father," "creator," and "Lord" might be so familiar as to be no longer metaphorical, what about, "a nail in a sure place," "a tried stone," "the breaker," and "your dread"?[8] All those metaphors come from the pages of the bible. However, the degree to which the latter four are recognizable may well depend upon more individual criteria, such as the portion of the Christian tradition most familiar to us. Even more clearly, the latter four continue to function as metaphors for most people. In other words, when we hear the phrase "God the breaker," it sparks a stronger response than "God the creator." That's because the word "creator" has been more absorbed into our concept of God.

As we shall see, there are dozens of different metaphors for the church, some of which still function, some of which have become labels, and some which have passed beyond labels into curiosities.[9] These images are extremely powerful. For instance, if the church sees its own role as setting moral and spiritual standards for the country, then it will address public issues in a very different way than if it is one more player in a marketplace of ideas. Similarly, a church that sees itself in terms of, "like a mighty army, moves the church of God,"[10] will behave differently than one that considers, "Come in, come in and sit down, you are a part of the

---

7. One list suggests 606 names in the KJV. See http://www.characterbuildingforfamilies.com/names.html.

8. Isa 22:23; Isa 28:16; Mic 2:13; Isa 8:13 (KJV).

9. It seems that the life cycle of the metaphor moves from being initially shocking, to familiar, to being absorbed as a statement of reality and then, in some cases, to historical curiosity.

10. "Onward Christian Soldiers," words by Sabine Baring-Gould, first published in the *Church Times*, 1865. The music for the hymn was called "St. Gertrude," and was composed by Arthur Sullivan in 1871.

family,"[11] to be its guiding metaphor. In this study, I explore many of the images in current use and suggest ways in which other metaphors might be more helpful.

I focus on the sub/urban church because it is different from its rural and small town cousins. It is neither better nor worse, simply different. The roots of those variations can be identified in tradition, history, and context. What is the nature of the Christian tradition that tends to preference rural and natural settings as opposed to urban and constructed? What is the history of the city, and the church in the city, in relation to faith and popular opinion? How does the context of the city church that brings it most directly into contact with anti-religious and areligious forces, and some of the extremes of wealth, poverty, opportunity, and deprivation in society, affect its mission?

For Reflection and Discussion

- Have you ever experienced a situation where a word meant different things to different people? What was that like?
- If you are part of a faith community/congregation/fellowship, what would you say are the distinguishing characteristics? Does being sub/urban make a difference? How would you describe that difference?
- When you think about "the city" from the perspective of faith, what comes to mind?
- What image(s) or word picture(s) best capture the church for you?

---

11. "Come in and Sit Down," words and music by James Manley, published in *Voices United*, 1996.

Chapter 1

The Situation

Constant One,

in our society, we are so used to the convenience of the disposable, throwaway items,

In our world, we are getting used to the idea of disposable people thrown on garbage heaps created by violence, greed and calamity.

Heal us of our life-destroying wastefulness.

Save us from soul-destroying indifference.

Prick our ears so that we may hear your voice.

intermingling with the groans of creation

And the cries of the dispossessed. Amen[1]

When you read the word "church," what comes to mind? The astonishing range of responses should serve as a reminder of the power of words. You might think of the institution, the building, and groups of people or specific individuals. You might call to mind certain activities. In most groups, there will be a range of emotions evoked by that one word "church." Sometimes illustration and imagination are more effective than argument and documentation. That is the intent of the following.

---

1. Hardy, *Worship in the City*, 110.

The Situation

Call to mind your favorite neighborhood restaurant. Reconstruct it in your mind as clearly as you can—sight, sound, and smell. In my chosen restaurant, the staff know me by name. Before I'm settled at my usual table my normal beverage is waiting. I love the food and the ambience. I can order a meal without glancing at the menu. The staff has even been known to take telephone messages for me. When your restaurant is fixed in your mind, consider three sets of circumstances.

In the first, your neighborhood has been levelled by an earthquake and you have been forced to flee your home. Thus, you know that even if you could return to your own home—which is by no means certain—and even if the restaurant were to be rebuilt, things would never be quite the same. We will label that experience, *exile*.

A second set of circumstances: in this case, you are now living in another community or perhaps in a foreign country. You're there for an extended stay to work or study. You are enjoying yourself even though you get a little homesick now and again. But, as you recall that favorite restaurant you know that when—not *if*, but *when*—you return your favorite table, your familiar food and that welcoming staff will all be there. We will call that experience, *sojourning*.

A final set of circumstances. Now you are still living in your own home and your favorite restaurant is still there. However, when you go there, the staff no longer recognizes you, you can't get a seat, and, if you should hang around long enough for a table, your preferred one is permanently occupied by someone else. The menu has changed, and you think you recognize some of the dishes, but you can't be entirely sure. We will call that experience, *displacement*.

As well as describing actual experiences, exile, sojourning, and displacement are all theological words. They can apply equally to physical reality and psychological and spiritual experiences. They are words that apply to the position of the church in its surrounding society. The concept of exile is familiar to readers of the Old Testament. It has been given a wider application through the writings of Walter Bruggemann.[2] In a variety of publications, he has advanced the concept of exile as a metaphor for the formerly mainline North American churches. It's an idea with strong appeal. It has a familiar ring for readers of the Old Testament. It's associated with generally positive terms like "Chosen People" and "Promised Land." When we forget the initially terrifying shock of being uprooted, it may even cause us to imagine that God is on our side. In the hands of some folks, it becomes the reason why we don't have the same social position as we enjoyed in the 1950s: some bad folks (and here you can insert various races, religions, and ideologies) have taken it away from us. And just as Israel looked forward to returning to its Promised Land, so too we can look forward to our own Promised Land.

It is an example of a powerful metaphor. To say, "the exile of the mainline church" is fresh enough that it arrests our attention. Neither "exile" nor "mainline church" has absorbed the other. Simply by being expressed, it evokes a range of responses. Certainly, Brueggemann cannot be blamed for the ways others have abused it. He appears to look forward to a *new* promised land, constructed by God, where the peace and justice so noticeably absent now will flourish. In the hands of some, the metaphor takes a very different form. Some authors pick up the idea of exile as punitive and use that to attack (in God's name) whatever group or change they oppose. The idea is that if we can somehow "get right with God," everything will return to what it was before the exile began. In many cases this sounds like the 1950s: a polite, middle class, alliance of church and state. A troubling vision of the Promised Land! When the metaphor is used this way, it has certain entailments: less diversity of race and religion; fewer opportunities for girls and women; greater authority for certain institutions; and a generally more restricted outlook on life.

Sojourn is a second powerful biblical metaphor, found most explicitly in the Letter to the Hebrews. There, the anonymous author of the letter writes of a long list of men and women who

2. See especially, Walter Brueggemann. *Cadences of Home: Preaching Among Exiles.* Louisville: Westminster John Knox, 1997.

The Situation

were heroes of the Old Testament. He then speaks of their persevering in seeking something better and the opportunities to give up on the search as well. The image concludes with the metaphor of a heavenly city prepared for them by God.[3] This is a powerful metaphor with strong antecedents in our spiritual family tree. Much of the overt theology from the spirituals that grew out of the African-American slave experience carried the sojourner motif: "I'm just passing through and this world is not my home."[4] This is a vital theme for Christians suffering persecution in many times and places (including our own). By the same token, it can promote a kind of Christian passivity where the focus is on future deliverance rather than confronting contemporary injustice. In terms of the members of formerly mainline congregations, sojourning as a metaphor would seem to blunt, rather than sharpen, our awareness and analysis of God's current call. Participants in those congregations are often comfortable, and indeed respected, in our society. Except in matters of faith and its expression, they are fully in step with the culture around them. Sojourning doesn't work as a metaphor.

What about displacement as a metaphor? As it is used here, it implies that we have remained in the same physical location and that most, if not all, of the features of the society around us remain unchanged. We go to that familiar restaurant and everything appears the same but is somehow different: the staff no longer know us, the menu has changed, and no one makes space for us. The circles of power and influence look much the same in the city but there's no place reserved for us. Instead, the church or its representatives are trotted out now and again to serve other people's agendas. Many clergy experience this at weddings and before banquets. It's called displacement.

---

3. Amongst other possibilities, see Heb 11:14–16.

4. We need to exercise caution about drawing too many "obvious" conclusions from the spirituals. Dolores Williams (Williams, "Rub Poor Lil' Judas's Head") makes a powerful case for the spirituals as a community's voice sharing a belief in language designed to conceal true meaning from the masters. However, even accepting her argument, many of the spirituals appeal to a vision beyond the suffering of this life. Relief is found elsewhere.

Consider the following evidence: In 1957, 75 percent of all Canadian Roman Catholics attended worship on a weekly basis. For the United Church of Canada, the figure was 40 percent, and for the Anglicans/Episcopalians, 27 percent. In 1993, those figures were: Roman Catholics, 27 percent; United Church of Canada, 20 percent; and Anglicans/Episcopalians, 16 percent. If the trends continue, the average will be about 15 percent by 2020. In the census of 2001, for the first time, "none" replaced "United Church" as the second most popular response for those who replied to the question on religious identification. We are no longer at the center of community life, much less the religious spectrum. That's been true for much longer than we have chosen to recognize. It's called displacement.

A congregation I once served occupies a beautiful 160-year-old building. It's the second home in their 260 plus years. For many of those years, they could rely on *obligation* to fill the pews and membership rolls. Attending church, being part of the church, and having your children "christened" in church were all part of a constellation of social obligations. Now, *motivation* has replaced obligation and folks come seeking value and experiences for themselves. In many cases, it seems that in the life of the obligation-congregation morality replaced grace, and the demand to be part of various "good works" (and they *were* good and important tasks) displaced the crucial elements of grace, new life, and forgiveness.

If the 1950s were the heyday of mainline religion (in that period my denomination broke ground on a new church-related building once a month, on average), the 1960s and 1970s were the era when trust and confidence in institutions was tested and, in many cases, shattered. There are many examples of authority being abused, and as a result, being ridiculed or dismissed outright. Where the orderly life of the 1950s was stifling and dehumanizing for many, the decades that followed were turbulent and troubled, and the civic faith of the mainline churches was often unable to respond. Those congregations had become associated with many of the structures that were being torn down and were experienced

The Situation

as offering a Christianity that was little more than good citizenship plus Sunday obligation.

Through this period, changes in legislation and policy meant that North America was transforming into a multi-cultural and multi-religious society. Where previous waves of immigrants had been largely European in background, now there were waves of visibly different individuals. As the decades progressed, these groups became increasingly vocal in their insistence that the much-celebrated rights and freedom of our country ought to extend to them as well. They were not prepared to remain ethnic curiosities. The mainline churches were often at the forefront of welcoming these newcomers and assisting in the journey of the most vulnerable refugees. At the same time, such congregations were less effective when it came to helping members give an account of their own faith and why they held it. That's part of the pluralistic reality for which we have been ill-equipped.

If we read the statements and reports of major Protestant denominations in this period, we see a curious mixture of concern and complacency. There was deep unease about many of the changes that were genuinely harmful to individuals, families, and communities. There were many valiant and creative attempts to respond to the different crises that change produced. At the same time, those who were most committed to responding found themselves caught between the suspicion of those who had lost trust in the churches, and those within the churches who complacently (or fearfully) wanted to leave it all alone. Despite the warning signs, there was a general tendency to assume that the place, relevance, constituency, and importance of the Protestant mainline would always exist.

Ronald Heifetz_ helpfully distinguishes between "technical work" and "adaptive challenges." At the risk of overly simplifying his analysis, technical work can be understood as defining a problem and developing a solution. The technical work in response to the baby boom was to build more churches and erect more and better-equipped education wings. Adaptive work, on the other hand, is less clear. The real problem may appear obvious only in some cases, but the solution requires learning and change. Adaptive work is what challenges the urban church today and our technical solutions often serve to make the problem worse.[5]

When I was growing up in Toronto all the stores were closed on Sunday. I can remember when the first movies were shown on Sunday. There were very few non-religious activities on Sunday and none in the morning. It seemed normal but, of course, it was a way in which society supported the church. I learned the Lord's Prayer in public grade school where opening exercises, including the national anthem and overtly Protestant moral lessons, were a daily experience. I could continue to list those cultural supports for Christianity, but you can probably create your own list. Consider the current reality. In most jurisdictions, Sunday shopping is the norm. There is a wide range of walks, marathons, and rallies for worthy causes. Sunday has become a "family day" filled with other activities as increasingly pressured families prepare to begin the rat race again on Monday. Of course, there are significant numbers of different religious experiences available as well.

The Protestant mainline churches (regardless of the length of their traditions) were creatures of modernity. We shared the confidence in self-sufficiency, reason, technology, progress and so on. I've been collecting sermons for a long time and when I look at those from my home congregation, where the clergy were some of the finest preachers of their generation, I am struck by the degree to which reason and religion go hand in hand in virtually every message. Now we face a new reality that is sometimes called "postmodernity." Some scholars have referred to the death of the "metanarrative": the overarching shared stories that gave meaning to society. There is no longer a single news narrative: you can choose from hundreds of channels and access newspapers and magazines from around the globe via the Internet. We have become much more aware that everyone dwells in a particular place with a certain set of experiences and influences. Much of that has been useful in dismantling an unhelpful parochialism. However,

---

5. Heifetz, *Leadership Without Easy Answers*. Cambridge: Harvard University Press, 1998.

The Situation

with its commitment to the middle-class narrative, the mainline church found it difficult to speak its faith in the new setting. That is an adaptive challenge.

It does allow for some fun though. Tony Robinson suggests that when someone says that they can't accept Easter because they're a modern person, he replies:

> Well yes, that's not surprising, you live in a closed world, a world that is fully explained and predictable. No wonder you have trouble with Easter, with the claim that God is breaking into the world, doing a new thing, that God can raise the dead. That is difficult for satisfied moderns. But take heart, with God all things are possible.[6]

These realities all tend to be more clearly visible in our secular, multi-faith and multi-ethnic cities. So, what is the church to do? Once again, there are various responses. Many congregations slip into a form of depression and assume that chaplaincy (primarily, funerals) is all their future holds. They blame their failure in the numbers games (that are so important in our society), the lack of spiritual interest in their neighbor's lives, or a greater degree of self-centeredness. These are offered as reasons to avoid the demanding task of self-examination and coming to terms with the new reality.

The postmodern individualism of the sub/urban center often challenges the formerly mainline churches. That individuality affects everything, including the way we read the bible. Originally written as a text to be read in the community, scripture is usually interpreted in extremely personal terms. However, a closer look at the city around us contains signs of hope that we often miss. For instance, cross-generational affiliation rates are high. In other words, if my parents were Roman Catholic or United Church, there is an 85 to 90 percent chance that I would identify myself that way, although the ways in which that translates into practice vary widely. Affiliation rates have even more significance when we recognize that repeated surveys show that folks are not lost in

---

6. Robinson, *Transforming Congregational Culture*, 23.

individualism but complain of the lack of adequate framework for faith's expression. The test of vitality in the twenty-first century includes a significant component of community,[7] but community understood in ways that are consistent with urban realities rather than rural memories.

    I live in a part of the country that tends to be more overtly respectful of institutional Christianity than other areas. Recently, at the time of the installation of a new Lieutenant-Governor of the province, there was a service of prayer and blessing for her, held in a local cathedral. It was a lovely service and quite sincerely meant, but I pondered at the time how extremely Christian it was. I couldn't help wondering about the statement such a service was making about the relationship of organized Christianity and government in my province. It was an Anglican (Episcopal) service and the Lt.-Governor is the Queen's representative. Why a Christian service and not an interfaith one?[8] Having been invited to pray over more than one newly-elected county council is an irony that I have participated in before. A more troubling example is the fact that the Lt.-Governor and the Premier (or at least their offices) are both patrons of the annual leaders' prayer breakfast which makes no attempt to even acknowledge the multi-faith reality of our province, much less participate in it. These are examples of displacement: in some ways, the old patterns of a power relationship seem to persist, and in others, they have disappeared. For instance, even as the elected head of the largest Protestant group in the Maritimes, I would have no more access to the government than any ordinary citizen. I hasten to add that I feel that is entirely proper. What I am pointing to is the irony—the sense of displacement—of being at one time considered important for inclusion and at most others on the outside looking in. That is a regular experience in urban ministry.

    7. Wuthnow, *Christianity in the Twenty-first century: Reflections on the Challenges Ahead.*

    8. The setting was made even more ironic by the fact that the new Lt.-Governor was the former head of the Human Rights Commission of the province, and was instrumental in instituting annual gatherings of religious leaders from all traditions.

THE SITUATION

For Reflection and Discussion

- How do you respond to the word "church"? Can you identify the source of your response?
- Reflect on your experiences of exile, displacement, and sojourn? What have those been like? What was the context for each experience?
- What public supports for religion can you remember that once existed and no longer do? Can you remember when they were removed and why? How do you feel about that change?
- What are your experiences of the response of faith communities to changing social contexts? Do those inspire you, depress you, or create a sense of ambivalence in you?

Chapter 2

Hymn and Biblical Metaphors for the Church

IF WE SUSPECT THAT many of the traditional metaphors for the church have lost some or all of their impact on sub/urban church participants, one of the places to begin our consideration is with the current selection. For that reason, this section examines the metaphors found in hymnody and scripture. In this study, it is important to keep in focus the purpose for which a metaphor is employed in the church. The two primary functions are inwardly- and outwardly-focused. In other words, some metaphors function to help the group identify themselves, one another, the community they form, and their core values. They may be used to name boundaries (who is in or out), qualifying experiences (everyone here shares a certain life occurrence), or the benefits/expectations of participation. Outwardly-focused metaphors serve a rhetorical or dogmatic/apologetic function by expressing the group's convictions vis-à-vis the surrounding context or some portion thereof. In drawing those contrasts, with the world around, such metaphors may also serve to invite individuals to leave that context and enter the church community. For example, the hymn, "Just as I Am," not only speaks of the loving reception of the sinner but invites the singer to reflect on the degree to which the words reflect her current life situation.[1]

Indeed, one of the ways in which mainline Protestants most clearly connect with the faith tradition is through hymns. For such folks, hymn texts (and the contexts they evoke in the singer's mind), rather than scripture passages, may well be more foundational in their theological formation. Of course, in reviewing any such resource, we must be conscious of the reflection of the editorial committee's theology in the music selected. Be that as it may, a review of a recent hymnbook[2] suggests the following areas of imagery for the church are evident:

1. There is a heavy emphasis on a gathered people in worship.

   - Sometimes the language is of invitation
   - Sometimes the language is of sacrament

2. The church is characterized as a community of people who serve God in the world through:

   - Risk-taking
   - Service
   - Education
   - Living as an "exodus people"

3. There are specific references to a flock and to a shepherd.

   1. "*Just as I Am*," words by Charlotte Elliott (1835), and music is "Woodworth" by William B. Bradbury and others (1849). Sample images: "Just as I am, and waiting not/To rid my soul of one dark blot;" "Just as I am, poor, wretched, blind;/ Sight, riches, healing of the mind;" "Just as I am, Thou wilt receive,/ Will welcome, pardon, cleanse, relieve;" "Just as I am, Thy love unknown/ Hath broken every barrier down."

   2. *Voices United: The Hymn and Worship Book of the United Church of Canada*, (Toronto: United Church Publishing House, 1996, 2000). It is worth noting that this resource continues to enjoy wide sales in Protestant denominations outside of the United Church and outside Canada (including the United States, Britain and Australia). A similar exercise with other denominational resources yields roughly similar results.

4. More overtly, theological concepts cluster around:

- A foretaste of the heavenly Jerusalem
- A glimpse of the kingdom
- Christ's new creation, with international scope, and existing both in trouble and to trouble the surrounding society

The most complete summary of biblical metaphors for the church is found in Paul S. Minear's, *Images of the Church in the New Testament*. There he identifies ninety-four images for the church in the second testament.[3] As we might expect with such an extensive list, some of the references are obscure indeed and one might quibble over the degree to which particular examples really are intended to evoke the church. Overall, however, it is an extremely useful resource for the purpose of testing the degree to which metaphors for the church can be said to have life in the experience of contemporary participants.

I've employed the list in Minear on two occasions. The first was approximately fifteen years ago with two small groups in two different congregations. The second was more recently with a current congregation when they offered them by email to a large group and invited replies. As a result, none of the claims advanced in this section can be represented in any sense as "scientific" in nature. However, these surveys do provide grist for some reflection. Most noteworthy is the fact that fewer than 50 percent of Minear's images evoked any recognition in the two surveys (although there was a slightly larger response in the earlier group which was more diverse theologically). In the later survey, I took the added step of inviting respondents to indicate images which had spoken to them formerly but do not do so now.

There were some striking similarities and differences in the two surveys.

- "Salt of the earth" was the favorite image in the early group; it was one specifically rejected in the later.

3. Minear, *Images of the Church*.

- Given the sizes of the surveys, "tree of life" was equally popular.
- "Followers" ranked relatively highly in early group but was rejected by as many as selected it later.
- Is there a parallel in the respondents' minds between the "household" and the "kingdom" of God that explains the relative popularity of those terms?
- Then there are the final four from the later survey which did not receive any recognition in the earlier.

Table 1

First Survey 24 respondents	Second Survey Formerly 2nd number indicates choice in first survey	Second Survey Currently 2nd number indicates choice in first survey
The salt of the earth (17)	Salt of the earth (4)	
The tree of life (15)		The tree of Life (7)
The people of God (14)		People of God (6)
Followers (13)	Followers (6)	Followers (6)
The household of God (14)		The Kingdom of God (10) (8)
Servants (14)		
Diversities of Ministries (14)		
	Twelve tribes (3) (3)	
	God's glory (4) (8)	
		Spiritual body (8) (13)
		Light (6) (7)
		The table of the Lord (7) (10)

In the same survey, I asked for definitions of common Christian words and received some interesting answers. What is truly fascinating is that when I correlate individuals' answers to what I (think I) know about them (there was a voluntary opportunity to self-identify), I really had no clue what was in their heads. A final observation can be summarized in the comment of one respondent: "Ouch. This was a scary exercise. I realize that 90 percent of the Church's vocabulary is dead to me and always has been." This is a lifelong church member.

Several observations related to our project are suggested at this point. The first is the sheer profusion of images. Certainly, ninety-four is a significant number, but the diversity in Minear's list also speaks to the fact that the New Testament authors had no hesitation in drawing images from virtually every realm and facet of life. Equally significant is the fact that there is no apparent inclination to reduce this profusion of images or to create a neat pattern. Part of that diversity of self-recognition stems from the fact that the authors located the uniqueness of their community outside themselves in God. Minear observes that the aim was not to create one superior image and that the images benefit from association with one another. The images in the New Testament "work" because of their impact on the ears of the writers and readers.[4] That conclusion begs the question of whether we ought to seek for images that "work" because of their impact on modern ears. The issue in question is not primarily one of better or worse but of effectiveness combined with accurate connection to the tradition of faith.

The words offered by the later survey respondents (see Table 4 below) fall into two categories: acceptable and rejected. In such an exercise, it is interesting that people would use their freedom to indicate an unacceptable option. In the acceptable category, the clear majority are active concepts. This implies that respondents understand the church as an active rather than a static concept, one that expresses its vocation through loving, hopeful service in a constantly changing context.

The words that respondents were asked to define were deliberately chosen to reflect the life and work of the church (see Table 5). There were two primary purposes for this: to develop a fuller, rounder image of the church, and to test for consistency within the "church" concept. Because these are substantial concepts and our tradition does not emphasize the memorizing of specific answers,

---

4. Unless otherwise noted, documentation for the assertions in this chapter can be found in the tables at the end of the chapter.

some degree of difference was anticipated and experienced. The data reveals the following:

Church: There was a general agreement on the concept of a "community of people" who have come together for specific purposes variously described as hope, walking together, and following the teachings of Christ. A second group of responses focused around the setting where these activities occur.

Bible: Responses to this term continued the emphasis on people, their experiences of God, their stories of faith, the act of preaching, and embodiment. The secondary responses clustered around the foundational nature of the text for the community.

Faith: This term evoked for people matters of belief/conviction which are beyond categories of logic and proof, and the life grounded or lived in response to those convictions. In other words, once again we have a mobile and flexible content rather than a static one.

Life: There was a broad division in the responses to this term, which is not surprising given the educational background of many of the respondents. The first group were generally biological in nature, referring to breath, the property of organisms, etc. The second (larger) group referenced terms such as "gift," "experience," "process," and "journey." In the terminology developed in the previous chapter, this division alerts us to the challenge of a purely descriptive response to a metaphor.

Study: Again, it is likely a reflection of the educational level of the group that the responses to "study" were positive, process-and exploration-oriented. The one surprising answer was, "Working your passage to salvation." Unfortunately, that was on one of the few anonymous returns because it would be fascinating to discuss with the respondent just what that means. Is it a reflection on the experience of study, the value of knowledge, and the significance of "correct answers," in relation to salvation or something entirely different?

Worship: This is the central activity in most people's experience of church. It is the most likely place where someone's church encounter begins. It is also the aspect of church life that receives the most attention and has the greatest common connection. As such, the range of understanding demonstrated in the responses is both heartening and intimidating. Several replies focus on the activities of worship (prayer, praise, giving thanks) and its assumed purpose (celebration, contemplation, ritual, and being with God). A couple of responses imply a quite moving importance of worship: "A momentary stay in confusion," and "Letting go of the daily grind and focusing on God and our walk in life."

Service: As expected, this word evoked two sets of responses. The first focused on the "worship service" and provided replies similar to the previous group. The latter addressed the subject of sharing time and resources for the enhancement of life. Interestingly, the word provoked a strong negative response from one person who associated with "guilt and drudgery" (particularly for women).

Witness: This is a word not widely employed in our mainline tradition. With the exception of one respondent who expressed distaste for the word, most of the responses clustered in the area of acting or living one's faith. This is consistent with the long-term mainline emphasis on actions over words but may also indicate another aspect of urban church life where metaphors that relate to traditional Christian language spark an unintended response.

Struggle: In the previous sections, we have explored the challenges that the new context of sub/urban ministry puts before us. Congregations will continue to wrestle with various ways of understanding and living out their calling. Most of the responses to this word were negative or neutral at best. Whether or not church members are prepared to associate "wrestling with doubts," or "tough challenges," with the life of faith will become a major concern for those congregations that wish to thrive.

Joy: In this case, we might be surprised that none of the respondents mentioned a specific religious or spiritual term. On the other hand, by correlating these responses with those given for worship and faith, we can suggest that joy may well be a response to those for these people.

Conclusions

From this survey of biblical and hymnodical metaphors, we see that there exists a profusion of possibilities even in the extant sources. Those who have shaped these metaphors have drawn them from virtually every area of human endeavour with no attempt to regularize or systematize the results. Clearly, some metaphors have had more traction than others in terms of breadth of acceptance in the tradition. Equally clearly, different metaphors have found varied receptivity in various branches of the Christian faith. This suggests that there is no metaphor that is, in and of itself, to be immediately ruled out of consideration. Indeed, the breadth of examples contained in the second testament pushes us to consider whether our day-to-day metaphors for the church are excessively limited and pallid. While it could be argued that a metaphor is inappropriate, clearly such an observation can be made only after careful consideration. There continues to be great freedom in the metaphors through which the church names and animates its life.

We have also seen, from both the biblical examples and the responses to them, and the freely offered possibilities and definitions, that the context of the believing community has a tremendous influence on whether a metaphor is acceptable or not. This evidence suggests that metaphors which are traditional (in the sense of being both biblical in origin and widespread in use) may be counterproductive in any given contemporary setting. As a consequence, the urban congregation wanting to spark new life through more vigorous metaphors needs to carefully consider the denotative weight of a choice.

For Reflection and Discussion

- Do you have a favorite hymn or song about the church? What images or metaphors does it employ? Why does it impact you as it does?

- The chapter discusses a couple of surveys conducted with church participants and others. These are described in subsequent pages. Try them and see your results. What do you learn?

IMAGES OF THE CHURCH (DIAGNOSTIC TOOL)

Introduction

One of the challenges of contextual theology today is finding images and metaphors that "work" for modern believers. As you probably know, there are many different word pictures for the church. One of the questions I wish to test is the degree to which these images continue to "speak" to believers. By "speak," I mean that an image has sufficient emotional impact that you could say: "Yes, that's what I mean when I say 'church,'" or "That's a word picture I can use to speak of my (ideal) church."

In his book, *Images of the Church in the New Testament* (pages 268-69), Paul S. Minnear identifies the following images from the New Testament. You are asked to respond to the images in the following fashion.

If an image does not speak to you now nor never has – leave the response space blank.
If an image spoke to you formerly (as a child or in later life) - mark the response 'F'
If an image speaks to you currently – mark the response 'N'
For those that speak to you most strongly add a '+' beside the 'N'
If an image produces a strong negative reaction – mark the response 'O'

If there are other images or word pictures that really "speak" to you and are not included, please feel free to include them and expand upon them to whatever degree you wish. The results of this survey will be used only in aggregate form. No opinions will be attributed to any individual without a separate request for permission.

[The table drawn from Minear then followed with several blank lines for the recording of other images]

Please define the following in a word or phrase:

- *Church*
- *Bible*
- *Faith*
- *Life*
- *Study*
- *Worship*
- *Service*
- *Witness*
- *Struggle*
- *Joy*

Optional
Your name:_____

Table 2: Images in Minear and Corresponding New Testament References.

Chapter titles:
Chapter 2–Minor Images of the Church
Chapter 3–The People of God
Chapter 4–The New Creation
Chapter 5–The Fellowship in Faith
Chapter 6–The Body of Christ

	Text		Text
Chapter 2		Chapter 3	
The salt of the earth	Matt 5:13	the people of God	1 Pt 2:9–10
A letter from Christ	2 Cor 3:2–3	Israel	Gal 6:15–6
Fish and fish net	Mk 1:17/ Matt 4:19	A chosen race	1 Pet 2:9
The ark	1 Pet 3:18–22	Twelve tribes	1 Cor 1:1–10
Unleavened bread	1 Cor 5:7	The patriarchs	Rom 15:8–10

One loaf	1 Cor 10:16–17	Circumcision	Rom 15:8–10
The table of the Lord	1 Cor 10:21	Abraham's children	Gal 3:9
The altar	Heb 13:10	The exodus	John 3:14
The cup of the Lord	Mark 10:35–45	House of David	Rom 1:3
Wine	Mark 2:22	Remnant	Rom 9:27
The branches of the vine	John 15	The elect	Luke 9:35
Vineyard	Matt 21:28–34	Flock	Luke 12:32
The fig tree	Luke 3:6–9	Lambs who rule	Rev 2:26–27
The olive tree	Rom 11:13–19	The Holy City	Rev 3:12
God's planting	1 Cor 3:9	The Holy Temple	Acts 17:24
God's building	1 Cor 3:9	Priesthood	Rev 1:6, 5:10
Building on the rock	Matt 16:18–19	Sacrifice	Heb 2:13
Virgins	Matt 25:1–13	Aroma	2 Cor 2:15
The messiah's mother	Rev 12:1–2	Festivals	1 Cor 5:7–8
The elect lady	2 John 1:1	A holy nation	1 Pet 2:9
The bride of Christ	2 Cor 11:1	Chapter 4	
The wedding feast	Rev 19:9	The new creation	2 Cor 5:17
Wearers of white robes	Rev 19:7	First fruits	1 Cor 15:20–23
The choice of clothing	Gal 3:27	The new humanity	Col 3:10
Citizens	Eph 2:19	The last Adam	1 Cor 15:21–22
Exiles	Heb 11:13	The Kingdom of God	Mark 1
The dispersion	Jas 1:1	Fighters against Satan	Eph 5

Hymn and Biblical Metaphors for the Church

Ambassadors	2 Cor 5:18–21	Sabbath rest	Rom 14:4
Hosts and guests	Rom 14:3	The coming age	Rev 1:9
The boat	Matt 8:23–27	God's glory	1 Thess 2:12
Chapter 5		Light	Rev 21:22–24
The sanctified	Acts 19	Life	Rev 3:1
The faithful	Acts 5:11	The name	Matt 2:24
Followers	Eph 4:20	The tree of life	Rev 22:1–5
Disciples	Rev 14:4	Communion in the Holy Spirit	Acts 2
Road	Acts 9:2	The bond of love	1 John 3
Coming and going	John 6:33	Son of Man	John 1:51
Witnessing community	Rev 12:17	Chapter 6	
Confessors	Rev 12:11	The body of life	Rom 5–8
Slaves	2 Cor 4:5	Members of Christ	1 Cor 6:12–20
Friends	John 15:15	The diversities of ministries	1 Cor 12:1–11
Servants	Mark 9:35	Spiritual body	Rom 7:4–6
"With . . ."	Rom 9:32/ Col 3:34	Head of the cosmic spirits	Col 1:20
Edification	Eph 4:7–12	Head of the church	Col 1:16
Household of God	1 Pet 4:17	The body of this head	Col 2:11
Sons of God	Matt 23:9	The unity of Jews and Gentiles	Col 3:9–13
Brotherhood	1 Pet 2:17	The growth of the body	1 Cor 1:24–28
Justified	1 Tim 3:16	The fullness of God	Eph 4:4–6

Table 3: Number of times a metaphor was selected

	Selection by Survey			Selection by Survey	
Chapter 2	1st	2nd	Chapter 3	1st	2nd
the salt of the earth	17	F4/N3/N+	the people of God	13	F2/N5/N+5
a letter from Christ			Israel		
fish and fish net			A chosen race		
One loaf	10	N/N+	A holy nation		
The ark			Twelve tribes	3	F3/N/O
Unleavened bread			The patriarchs		
one loaf			circumcision	6	F2/O
the table of the Lord	10	F2/N2/N+5	Abraham's children	4	F2
The altar			The exodus		
The cup of the Lord			House of David		
Wine			remnant	8	F2
Branches of the vine	6	F2/N/N+	The elect		
Vineyard	4	F/N	Flock		
The fig tree			lambs who rule	5	F/O2
The olive tree			The Holy City		
God's planting			The Holy Temple		
God's building			Priesthood		
Building on the rock	10		sacrifice		
Virgins	1	F2/O3	Aroma		
The messiah's mother			festivals	7	N/N+

the elect lady	9	O2			
The bride of Christ			Chapter 4		
The wedding feast			the new creation	9	F/N3/N+
wearers of white robes	10	F2/O	First fruits		
the choice of clothing	2	O	the new humanity		F2/N/N+
Citizens	4	F/N+	The last Adam		
Exiles	7	F2/N/O	the Kingdom of God	8	F2/N4/N+6
The dispersion			Fighters against Satan		
Ambassadors	10	F/N2/O2	Sabbath rest		
hosts and guests		F2/N	The coming age		
			God's glory	8	F4/N4/N+
			Light	7	N2/N+4
			Life	8	N3/N+3
			The name		N2/N+
			the tree of life	15	F2/N5/N+2
			communion in the Holy Spirit	11	F/N/N+4
			the bond of love	14	N3
Chapter 5			Chapter 6		
The sanctified		N	the body of life	3	N4/N+
the faithful	11	F3/N/N+|2	members of Christ		F/N2/N+
Followers	7	F6/N4/N+2	the diversities of ministries	14	F/N2/N+2
Disciples	8	F4/N2/N+	spiritual body	13	F/N6/N+2
Road	10	F	Head of the cosmic spirits		

coming and going	6		Head of the church			
witnessing community	11	F/N3/N+	The body of this head			
confessors			The unity of Jews and Gentiles			
Slaves			The growth of the body			
Friends	9	F4/N4/N+	the fullness of God	6		N2/N+2
Servants	14	F2/N2/N+				
"with...	9					
edification	2					
household of God	14	F/N4				
Sons of God	3					
brother-hood	6	F3/N2/O				

Table 4: Additional images added in the second survey

Journey (This has become an increasingly important word for me in the context of faith as I age, watch things change, watch my reactions change, see my priorities change, etc.)
Service (To me this word implies giving one's time and talent to others and, by extension, to God.)
Ministry (I think many lay people consider their involvement in the church to be a ministry, especially if they use particular talents and skills in the service of the church.)
Voice of Hope (I would like to find images of the notion that the church is a community that embodies hope in the face of oppression, suffering, and a precarious future for the earth. I realize that means reclaiming hope as more than wishful thinking or Polyanna-ism.)
Love (not bond of)
Sanctuary
Body of Christ
Chosen Few (a formerly now quite negative)
An Institution (a present but negative)

Table 5: Definitions of words given in second survey

Church	-The body of people who by word and action try to live the life Christ wants us to live, and who find and act on some sense of community in this endeavor. Lots of people live a good life anyway but I believe the world needs a visible community as a foundation. It's better to build on a rock. -Community of faith -A group of people with a common approach to worship -Community of people who try to follow the teachings of Christ -A community of citizens who choose to walk together -Community of those who hope -Organization bringing together people of faith -Community of believers -Community of believers -Those who seek to understand the teachings of Jesus and apply them in everyday life -Community who strives to understand -A gathering place to participate and share in worship, prayer and song -A place of worship or the group of people sharing Christianity -A place to worship God

Bible	-The stories and history that sustain faith
	-Descriptive (and prescriptive) book of Christianity
	-The word of God
	-The starting place
	-Stories of people's relationships to God
	-The revelation of God when preached and embodied in a believing community (otherwise an interesting ancient document)
	-Historical opinion, reflection and account of the life of Jesus and God in the world
	-Historical reference
	-Collection of Inspiring stories
	-A library of faith in historical contexts
	-Basis of our faith
	-The book of God
	-The Word of God; a collection of sacred writings
	-Historical religious

Faith	-The mix of hope/certainty in God and the belief in the innate goodness of people and the world that empowers us
	-What we believe without proof
	-Belief in the Father, Son, and Holy Ghost
	-Belief in action
	-Moving in trust to a higher being/force
	-Response to God's love flooding our hearts
	-Belief in common good and living in community with others
	-Believing
	-Bottom line by which I live
	-Awareness of God's spirit and a willingness to respond
	-Trusting
	-Your belief in God and what is good in the world
	-Belief or confidence in God (or a person or inanimate object) which is not related to logic or reason
	-What grounds my being

Life	-The time we are given to use our talents as best we can
	-Positive energy
	-Not dead and existing here on earth
	-Anything that breathes
	-Breathing
	-A gift
	-Created embodiment of God's love
	-A journey in community with others worldwide
	-Influence of doingness
	-Precious gift, now and forever
	-Journey
	-Ever-changing; a learning experience
	-Engaging in a rich and meaningful process
	-A property of organisms that has a capacity to grow and react to stimuli
	-Precious and wonderful

Study	-Looking inward to explore questions of faith
	-Attempts or acts to gain more knowledge or understanding
	-Acquiring knowledge
	-Learning through reflection and research
	-Working your passage to salvation
	-Authentic pursuit of meaning
	-Learning and enhancing understanding, knowledge and skills
	-Learning
	-A continuum of inquiry
	-Focusing on learning
	-To work hard at something
	-Increase one's knowledge of a subject
	-Learning

Worship	-Coming together to pray, praise, and recommit to faith and action
	-Celebration
	-Individual or with a collective in prayer
	-The act of giving thanks
	-The experience of being with God
	-Community ritualization of the response to God's love
	-Reflection on enhancing global communities
	-Give praise to
	-A momentary stay in confusion
	-Gaining perspective and meaning through ritual and contemplation
	-Letting go of the daily grind and focusing on God and our walk in life
	-Being with God
	-The act of praise, honor or devotion through prayers, devotion, hymns
	-Peaceful contemplation

Service	-Doing the right thing unselfishly
	-Assuming as in "worship service," the time for worship (as above), study, and recommitting. If "Christian Service" is meant, then daily living with Christian Principles the basis for all actions
	-An organized time to worship
	-The act of living the word
	-Organized experience
	-(I really hate this word!!) guilt and drudgery (for women)
	-Sharing of gifts and talents to enhance global communities
	-Give self to
	-The basic mandate by which Christians live
	-Consciously trying to make the world better by treating all others with respect
	-Making life better for others
	-A responsibility, commitment to something worthwhile
	-An organized event in which the members worship
	-Organized worship

Witness	-Being able to speak personally of God's presence and grace
	-Telling the Christian story–generally from a personal perspective
	-To take responsibility
	-Staying true to Jesus' teachings
	-To see
	-Living gratitude
	-I have never liked this word
	-Be in observance of
	-Courage to tell the truth
	-Modelling Jesus' teachings
	-Others seeing my faith ad beliefs in action
	-Being part of something bigger than one's self
	-The way one lives/behaves/acts out one's faith or belief
	-Representing your belief & faith

Struggle	-Wrestling with one's own doubts, unbelief, misdeeds
	-Life
	-A difficulty trying to resolve a situation
	-Conflict
	-Work
	-Coping with the ambiguity of life
	-Internal and external conflict
	-Have difficulty with
	-Admission that life's questions are complex
	-Awareness of the gap between good intentions and actual achievements; the self vs. the ideal
	-Something that an individual feels/views and a difficulty or "bump in the road"
	-Participating in a difficult process
	-Fighting or resisting something unpleasant
	-A tough challenge

Joy	-Uplifted, reassured
	-Moments of self-actualization when a special calmness overcomes and trumps all struggles
	-An expression of happiness
	-Pleasure
	-The celebration of living
	-Peaceful acceptance of life
	-Freedom of thought and action
	-Raising of spirits
	-Sometimes a surprise and sometimes a determined choice
	-Joy; acceptance; harmony of self and sense of one's place in the world; loving and being loved.
	-That feeling of elation you feel in your head and chest; clarity
	-Day to day life with my children and family
	-Delight, pleasure
	-Confidently flying
	Ouch! That was a scary exercise! 90 percent of the church's vocabulary is dead to me—always was!

Chapter 3

The Challenge of Self-Understanding

3.1 SECULARIZATION AND THE CITY

Guide us, O God,
Amidst the commercial canyons and the insistent crowds
walking with grim purpose to their workplaces and shopping places.
In the busyness of the city, teach us to notice
the men and women on the margins,
the patches of green hidden in the courtyards,
the laughter as well as the desperation,
the places of healing and prayer.
Grant us
the ability to open our eyes to all that is around us,
the joy of life with friends and strangers of all races and abilities,
the caring that unlocks our fears and enables us to reach out to the world with love.[1]

WORDS ARE MORE THAN vocabulary and grammar. Words both carry and shape meaning. Sometimes those meanings are

---

1. Hardy, *Worship in the City*, 129.

denotative—the literal and primary sense of the word is what we want to convey. But when the discussion is about important subjects, the words carry important connotative meanings. In other words, they have emotional and cultural weight. So, if I say to you, "That building is a church," assuming you speak English, you'll catch the denotative meaning: it's a building where people gather for certain ritual or other purposes. But the same phrase has connotative meanings and your reaction is based on a host of factors. You might respond: "Well it doesn't look much like a church," based on a whole range of factors that contribute to the concept of "church" in your mind.[2]

A similar phenomenon occurs with the bible. Even if we can be assured of an accurate denotative translation, the text may carry a connotative burden that only knowing the meaning of words cannot encompass. For instance, in Luke 11:15–32,[3] an understanding of the social system of honor and shame that dominated first century Palestinian village life profoundly affects our comprehension and appreciation of the account.[4] It also demonstrates that there is no "meaning" that can be abstracted from the story. Rather, the meaning is found within the parable, even while not being exhausted by it. The radical contrasts and concrete images we find in the tale are not embellishments *on* the meaning; rather *they are the* meaning and it cannot be reached without them.

---

2. In the region of central Turkey known as Cappadocia there is a valley in which some 360 churches have been carved into the soft rock. Although a significant number have been damaged by earthquakes, several magnificent specimens remain. Almost all of them have "pillars": in other words, more or less upright columns. However, these columns are rarely at ninety degrees to the floor and are not load bearing. In other words, the carvers had the idea that a "real church" has columns and included them in these churches whether they were needed or not.

3. This parable is often called "The Prodigal Son," which is in itself an interpretation carrying a connotative meaning.

4. Cf., Bailey, Kenneth, E. *Poet and Peasant / Through Peasant Eyes: A Literary-Cultural Approach to the Parables in Luke*. Eerdmans: Grand Rapids, 1983. Rohrbaugh, Richard. "A Dysfunctional Family and its Neighbors: Luke 15:11–32." In *Perspectives on the Parables: Images of Jesus in his Contemporary Setting*, edited by G. Shillington, 141–64. Edinburgh: T. & T. Clark, 1997.

The Challenge of Self-Understanding

In many of our sub/urban churches, the images, symbols, sounds, narratives, and forms on which the church bases its worship do not connect with the lives of the participants.[5] What McFague says about God is equally true of the church: "It is not a question of being sure of God while being unsure of our language about God. Rather we are unsure both at the experiential and the expressive levels."[6] As we shall see, many of the metaphors and images used for the church are based on locations and ways of life (often rural and archaic) that have no connection to urban worshippers. As a result, church members must struggle to overcome the sense that Christian faith is properly confined to a narrow sphere of life, more as a matter of personal interest than of core identity.

There are other categories and metaphors in scripture that might have greater relevance in the city. For example, strangeness, being the stranger, and care for the stranger (by God and community) are themes extensively explored in the bible and routinely experienced in the urban church. These categories, which may engender fear, form a regular part of city ministry. Ministry in the city is tough: the city we love is often the city we hate. Therefore, we need to create language and symbols for that context. What does a beautiful phrase like "the Lord is my shepherd" mean in a context devoid of shepherds and sheep? In many sub/urban churches, Thanksgiving decorations are dominated by items brought in from the country: wheat sheaves, pumpkins, apples, and the like. How do those symbols help city dwellers to express gratitude to God in their context? By contrast, an African-American church devised its own symbols: a whiskey bottle, a lynch rope, and a crutch as signs of brokenness. Does the cross really belong in the middle of those symbols?[7]

As an experienced pastor, I think I've lost most of my illusions about rural and sub/urban life. Certainly, most of the challenges we associate with sub/urban life are present there as well. In

---

5. Meyers, *Envisioning the New City*, 156.
6. McFague, *Metaphorical Theology*, 1.
7. Meyers, *Envisioning the New City*, 198.

the city, however, the concentration of population with different forces and influences causes these realities to be more evident. For instance, poverty in the form of women and men living on the street and panning to make ends meet directly confronts the sub/urban pedestrian. The gathering of numbers of people in a smaller geographic area provides support for lifestyles or commitments which might be ostracized elsewhere. Patterns of immigration are such that, in general, the multi-cultural and multi-faith nature of sub/urban society is both more pronounced and visible. Because there are other options for the community and support functions provided by the rural church, many feel no need for organized religion in their lives at all.

Honesty compels us to acknowledge that some of the assumptions about the city which are often repeated as fact (and may indeed be most firmly held by city-dwellers), are mostly fanciful or based on limited experience. Harvie Conn does a fine job of exploring these misunderstandings, so we'll only note them in passing here.[8]

1. *The rural-urban myth.* This is the sense that anything goes in the city, particularly that which would not be experienced or allowed in rural areas. "It's the city, what do you expect?"

2. *The depersonalization misunderstanding.* Some people, especially those moving from close-knit rural communities, may feel that they are no longer individuals but merely numbers in the sub/urban sea. This misses the fact that the city is actually comprised of countless communities and people may find their identity in several different places.

3. *The crime generalization.* A popular misperception of sub/urban areas as dangerously crime-ridden is based on (a) a greater concentration of people, and (b) largely urban-biased media reporting. Crime rates *per capita* tend to be consistent across society.

---

8. Conn, *A Clarified Vision for Urban Mission: Dispelling the Urban Stereotypes*. Grand Rapids: Zondervan, 1987.

4. *The secularization myth.* We will consider this in detail, but there is a widespread understanding that faith is corroded simply by being exposed to the city.[9]
5. *The privatization generalization.* Many people are intimidated by the size of the city and put off by the resultant behaviors. When I returned to the city after several years of rural ministry, I realized that I was getting a headache from trying to make eye contact with everyone on the transit system. In our rural village, if you didn't at least acknowledge (if not engage) passersby, you'd hear about it next Sunday morning. In the city, that level of engagement is psychically impossible. Urban life is built upon different expectations of interaction with others.
6. *The power misunderstanding*: "You can't fight city hall." The sheer size of the sub/urban reality leads some to assume that the levers of power and decision are inaccessible to the ordinary citizen. In fact, local city councilors and staff members will attest that those who want to contact them do. As well, in the city, it may indeed be easier to gather the critical mass of companions to effect a change.
7. *The monoclass generalization*: "There's no one but poor folk in the city." This may be more of an American than a Canadian assumption. Experience suggests that the concentrations of need that we are associating with *urban mission* tend to dominate the urban cores of American cities more than Canadian. As well, those significant concentrations of poverty that do exist in every Canadian city are rarely in the immediate downtown core. Currently however, while both nations experienced the "white flight" to the suburbs, many cities are undergoing an economic revitalization of core housing. This is so much the case that the "gentrification" of rooming houses and whole neighborhoods places strain on the already

---

9. Mircea Eliade described sub/urban life as "the second fall of man." Gomez and Van Herk, *The Sacred in the City*, 55–56.

limited stock of affordable housing and causes the displacement of the economically marginalized.

Any discussion of the identity of the city church must address the question of secularization. The 1990s marked the end of a century in which both the demise of organized (Christian) religion and its absolute triumph had been proclaimed with equal fervour. In the latter part of the century particularly, leaders and writers supportive of the church spent a great deal of energy analyzing and interpreting this phenomenon. Much twentieth century socio-theological writing assumed that more modernization equaled less religion. Conversely, in those societies where religion was more dominant, it was anticipated that industrialization (and other aspects of "modernization") would proceed more slowly. As the theory went, when religion lost control over areas such as politics, health care, education, and economics, its role would become increasingly narrowly focused and unimportant to the general population.

By the end of the century, those equations and expectations had proven empty. Some of the most modern (i.e., technologically advanced) societies, such as the United States and Japan, were amongst the most overtly and publicly religious in their behavior. Indeed, Europe seemed the only region to follow the secularism model, an appearance strongly disputed by some scholars.[10] Major proponents of the secularism theme, such as Peter Berger and Harvey Cox, had been compelled to rethink their predictions.[11]

This poses a genuine challenge for formerly mainline churches. Secular means "not religious, sacred or spiritual." Secularism, however, has generally been restricted to the gradual diminution of organized religion's popularity and authority. Thus, the statistics quoted above regarding declining worship attendance in Canada

---

10. Hobsbawm, *The Age of Extremes*, 558. Cox, "The Myth of the Twentieth Century," 135–43.

11. Cox, *Fire from Heaven*, xvi. Berger, *Desecularization of the World*, 2. Berger makes the interesting point that we continue to hear about secularization because academic, legal, and media elites *have been largely secularized* and, therefore, project that position on the world which they report.

would be interpreted as evidence of increased secularism. Diminished attendance has certainly been the experience of the mainline churches in Canada (and much of the United States). Fewer people attend worship and they do so with less regularity. However, there is no evidence of less interest in the sacred or the spiritual. Indeed, in a recent book by Reginald Bibby, Canada's foremost tracker and interpreter of religious trends is compelled by the evidence to change his, formerly gloomy, prognostications about the future of organized religion in Canada.[12] Similar studies in the United States reveal that, while the popularity of religion (as measured by factors such as attendance and finance) has certainly declined, it would be an error to assume that all congregations of all denominations are in retreat.

The growing disillusionment with the idea of secularization should not be interpreted as a first-class ticket to the "glory days" of mainline religion in the 1950s. It is important to understand the relationship between the secularizing trend and the contemporary challenges to the church. Cox writes that secularism:

> tries to expel God and quarantine religion in the heart of the individual... the dilemma now is no longer to revive a comatose piety in an age of unbelief, but to cope with fresh voices of faith that do not conform to old patterns. Church leaders are faced not with a decline is spirituality but with a new outburst of religious energy.[13]

This new reality raises a variety of challenges for the formerly mainline churches. Since city residents tend, in many ways, to be more individualistic, less formal, less respectful of traditional institutions, and have a wider variety of options than their rural counterparts, these realities are magnified for urban churches. In the first place, this new spiritual interest is very much individually-driven. In other words, people are seeking answers to *their* questions as the major (and perhaps sole) priority. That individual focus, combined with the sheer number of questions being raised,

---

12. Bibby, *Restless Gods: The Renaissance of Religion in Canada*. Toronto: Stoddart, 2002.

13. Meyers, *Envisioning the New City*, 200.

renders ineffective the traditional mainline strategy of appealing to the widest number possible within the constraints of doctrine and resources. In other words, many of these searchers are unwilling to support an institution that is not answering their current questions, in the hope that it may do so someday, *unless* that organization shows that it is seriously trying to wrestle with participants' concerns. In that case, some seekers *may* be willing to wait awhile, in hopes that their question will become the focus.

A second major challenge for the church in the current context is that many spiritual searchers simply do not conceive of the church as a resource for their quest. The church struggles with the reputation of overwhelming concern for its own agenda and only addressing specific questions to which it already possesses an answer. As a result, many spiritual searchers consider the church irrelevant to their search.

This feeds into a third challenge, specifically around leadership. With only small course corrections now and again, the church and seminaries have prepared, and the local congregations have expected, leadership that can meet most of the needs of the majority of the congregation. However, the skills of a previous era are very different than the new one. Indeed, many of the assumptions underlying several generations of clergy training are counterproductive in this new era. Furthermore, the institutional expectations of the denomination around form and order may, in many cases, militate against the freedom and flexibility needed in the current context.

Given these factors (and the destructive practice of measuring institutional health through numbers: attendance, membership, and financial) it is not surprising that there is a sense of despair in many congregations. The hard truth is that many of our sub/urban centers are over-churched, if by that we mean a physical capacity predicated on previous assumptions of church-going. Put bluntly, in an era when church attendance is far more optional, and indeed counter-cultural, than it was one or two generations ago, we simply have too many seats seeking too few bottoms. The mainline church has been displaced in our society. But what if sub/urban churches were to take seriously the freedoms and the challenges of our displacement? We are, perhaps for the first time since the New Testament Book of Acts,[14] competitors in a marketplace of ideas. In that competition of convictions, the local urban congregation has significant resources if they can be identified and released. First, though, we must see and accept the truth.

THE CHALLENGE OF SELF-UNDERSTANDING

3.2 Contextual Theology

> Holy God, creator of all that lives and breathes,
> comforting God who cares for us
> like a strong mother and a gentle father,
> this day we begin our yearly journey,
> remembering Christ's choice
> to suffer with those
> who taste the ashes of rejection and scorn;
> whose choice led
> to death at the hands of the powerful.
>
> Suffering God, you who see and know,
> you who love and forgive,
> to you we raise our lament
> that violence and hatred
> hunger and greed and death
> still choke and stifle the lives
> of your beloved children.[15]

For the local church, the purpose of theology is to aid in the hearing and living of the gospel. Today, there are enormous challenges to accomplishing that task. Under previous paradigms (such

---

14. A crucial scripture for the contemporary sub/urban church is found in Acts 17:16–23, recalling Paul in debate with representatives of other philosophies in Athens.

15. Hardy, *Worship in the City*, 88.

as Christendom), the arguments of German-and English-speaking theologians in Europe, Britain, and North America were accepted as applying to "everyone." Of course, as feminist and other contemporary theologies have taught us, the phrase "everyone knows" really applies only to the outlook of those who have the power to shape discourse. Classical theology understood its subject as an objective reality. Difficult and mysterious, at times, and never fully articulated, theology was understood as addressing an objective reality separate from the author and the believer. For much of the twentieth century for Protestants, belief meant intellectual assent to certain propositional statements. Increasingly, however, we are seeing the rise of contextual theologies. These are unabashedly subjective. That does not mean that they are relative or private. It does mean that humans—rather than some abstracted principle(s)—are the source of reality. Of course, those human beings and their society are broken and disordered in many different ways and that turmoil affects our perception. Nonetheless, contextual theology insists that it is this reality (rather than some objective state) that is available to us. It is in this, often highly ambiguous world, that we live the life of faith.

Traditional theology would immediately fix such a claim with concerns about truth and falseness. That paradigm was convinced there was an identifiable "truth" that applied to all people, contexts, and times (or at least most of them). "Subjective" was (and remains for many) a dismissive term used for those who were unwilling or unable to cope with the demands of the truth. The great danger of a subjective theology was that it would relativize "truth," sweeping the foundations from under universal doctrines. What contextual theology declares is that we can still label theological insights as "true" and "false." In this case, however, a false theology is one that does not honestly reflect its time and context. Of course, this has been true from the outset for Christians as neither biblical testament has a single theology, let alone a theology for the entirety of the bible.[16]

---

16. Bevans, *Models of Contextual Theology*, 2–4.

The Challenge of Self-Understanding

Contextual theology poses a couple of major challenges for the sub/urban congregation; at the same time, it opens significant possibilities. In the congregation where members are predominantly from the social mainstream, many participants will unreflectively share the same assumptions concerning the universality of objectivity and truth. Furthermore, particularly from the more doctrinaire spokespeople of religion (not exclusively Christianity), there is a constant bombardment of "truth." While rejecting much of the content of that barrage, many mainline Christians still hold to the notion that "truth" can be identified—it's just not what *they* say it is. There is also the legitimate concern for a means to determine beliefs and practices that are more deeply rooted than merely our convenience and happiness. If we acknowledge from the outset our capacity to delude ourselves and others, what standards can we apply besides, "It just feels right"? Stephen Bevans suggests three tests we can apply. Since these are the tests we will be applying to the sub/urban theology laid out in this study, let us examine them in some detail.[17]

Bevans' first test is an orientation in the same direction as other successful or approved theologies. Contextual theologies are not isolated acts of Christian reflection. Rather, they are specific moments in a vast stream of Christian contemplation and action. As such, any contextual theology that is developed needs to be in dialogue with rest of the tradition. That does not mean identical or in slavish agreement (or else why would one bother to go to the effort?), but in coherent conversation with what has gone before and is occurring currently. Thus, while the New Age movement contains many examples of Gnosticism,[18] a contextual theology that advanced Gnostic ideas or practices as its foundation would not be "truly" Christian because it is oriented away from virtually every other theology that has found ongoing life in the community of faith. On the other hand, the categorization of "finding ongoing life" leaves a lot of room for doctrinal creativity.

---

17. Bevans, *Models of Contextual Theology*, 18.

18. See for example the phenomenally popular *Celestine Prophecy* series of books and studies.

The second test is that the contextual theology proposed leads to actions that conform to a view of Christian orthopraxis. Orthopraxis is a word that comes to us from liberation theology. Whereas "orthodoxy" is a common Christian word meaning "right belief," liberation theologians wish to emphasize the expression of Christianity in daily living and social organization. To distinguish this from ordinary routine behavior they coined the word orthopraxis, where praxis is behavior we have reflected upon. There is no consensus about what constitutes either orthodoxy or orthopraxis. However, as a general test of a contextual theology, a concern for orthopraxis directs us to whether followers of that theology are led toward greater active care for God, neighbor, and self.

If the first test compels dialogue with the Christian family through time, the third test demands interaction with Christian contemporaries and, in an increasingly pluralistic society, all people of good will. Bevans insists that a valid contextual theology will have "proper reception or acceptance by the people of God." This by no means implies total agreement. One of the characteristics of lasting theologies through the ages is that those for whom Christian thought is important deemed them worthy of debate. A further feature is the existence of those who were prepared (at some level) to live out the insights offered. Put bluntly, people buy the book and try and put it into practice. A contextual theology that finds no acceptance or adoption amongst God's people remains, at best, an interesting theory.

Why is a contextual theology needed for the sub/urban congregation? Because (as we are seeing) the sub/urban church is different and needs its own resources for faithful life and mission. For instance, there is the common risk of confusing an idealized rural life with the Christian *koinonia*. We need ways of relating the gospel in a meaningful manner to the sub/urban area. Such a theology must come to terms with the fact that "community" in the city has its own demands. If we employ the common law-gospel distinction, the "law" is the driving conformity that the city exercises in so many ways to accept others' choices for us. From the media to the peer group to the local politicians, the city is replete with pressures to accept the idea that what others tell us ought to be important, and truly will be so for us. In this context, "gospel" is the summons to make choices and accept the responsibility for those choices.

That includes the way we deal with people. Rurally-based notions of community are impossible to sustain in the city. You cannot make eye contact with everyone—and probably shouldn't. "Cities are full of people with whom, from your viewpoint, or mine, or any individual's, a certain degree of contact is useful or enjoyable; but you do not want them in your hair. And they don't want you in theirs either."[19] That list includes the variety of service people one encounters in a day: perhaps the person you regularly pass in the coffee shop, the individual who lives on your block, maybe the person in another department in your firm. Martin Buber is famous for his distinction of "I-Thou," suggesting that if the other was not in the category of "Thou," we were utterly ignoring them.[20] In the city we *must* have a category of "other" or "it" that encompasses a relationship which is, at one and the same time, respectful and neither deeply personal nor utterly impersonal. There must be a category of people whom we can enjoy without being in their hair.[21]

The Role(s) of the Sub/Urban Church

The sub/urban church can play several vital roles in the life of the city. One has to do with the creation and maintaining of community. A second, and increasingly crucial function, is to speak the truth. Karl Barth told us to read with the bible in one hand and the newspaper in the other. This is wise counsel for a Christian faith that is securely grounded in God's world of human interactions with one another and the rest of creation. However, in an era of increasingly centralized control of the various media there is a new

19. Jacobs, *The Death and Life*, 56.
20. Buber, Martin. *I and Thou*. Translated by R. G. Smith. Edinburgh: T. & T. Clark, 1950.
21. Northcott, *Urban Theology*, 71.

and more insidious double-headed challenge. On the one hand, the various organs of public media are held in increasingly fewer hands and reflect a centralized editorial philosophy. In that case, the "news" is presented as evidence for an already-determined position which establishes not only what will be reported but how it will be set out. On the other hand, the explosion of the Internet provides for a level of personal expression to a mass audience that is unprecedented in human communication. The issue then is to sort out reliable and useful sources within the tsunami of websites available. More recently we have been made aware of the prevalence of "fake news"—stories generated in clear opposition to fact and circulated as if true. Their credibility is established through viral repetition in social media. The effect is that the average person receives the story from multiple sources and, therefore, ascribes truth to it, without being aware of its original, single-source origin. This is such a powerful phenomenon that the editors of the prestigious Oxford Dictionary declared "post-truth" as the word of the year for 2016.[22] In a "post-truth" society, the sub/urban church can have a profound role in opposing the many forms of false proclamation which are generally geared toward nativism, hatred, fear of the stranger and the marginalized, and other counter-gospel values.

Most people continue to rely on the public media. Regardless of what one chooses as a source of record, chances are that establishment interests have already cleansed the material to protect us from the truth of the street.[23] Much of the "theology" that permeates the public sphere is exceedingly establishment in nature, defends the status quo, and suggests that any other foundation leads to an irrational and irresponsible conclusion. The sub/urban church, in its independent status and strength of faith and community, can respond to the false speech: the propaganda of the state, the exaggerations of Bay or Wall Street, the twisted commitments of politicians, the claims of expertise by bureaucrats, the

22. https://en.oxforddictionaries.com/word-of-the-year/word-of-the-year-2016.

23. Saunders and Campbell, *Word on the* Street, xii.

The Challenge of Self-Understanding

subtle lies of racism, and the diversion of entertainment. However, in order to take up that calling, the sub/urban faith community must first deal with a metaphor offered by Martin Luther King Jr.: "The church has become a thermometer rather than a thermostat, recording the climate around it rather than changing it."[24] The constant call to the sub/urban church—the very hope of the city—is found in Amos' challenge to determine the difference between good and evil and make a choice.[25]

As will be made explicit later in this study, the justice-seeking and truth-stating work of the sub/urban church is best done in collaboration with other groups. The days are long past when, on their own, or even in collaboration only with other churches, the ecclesiastical structures could make an impact on our society. Today's justice seekers come from a range of backgrounds and organizations. The city congregation brings to the conversation a continuity of expression. Those in non-church groups often live split lives, with a foot in one organization and the other in some sort of group. Such groups often run the risk of pride, believing that they are somehow an elite exercising a role that is reserved for the few. The sub/urban church that is firmly rooted in its community brings to the table the reminder that the remnant is not created for the sake of the few but in order that all might be more authentic.

A sub/urban church that is genuinely rooted in its surroundings and in its scriptures, will be committed to hearing the voice of God in the cries of the oppressed. A biblically-formed people will recognize the unreality of so-called "neutrality." Christians who have read their scriptures know that God is not neutral, for such "objectivity" amounts to a reinforcement of the status quo. When the sub/urban congregation first enters public domain issues, an establishment response might be to condemn the church for "taking sides." What has in fact happened is not a choosing of sides,

---

24. Brown, *Theology in a New Key*, 156.

25. Amos 5:15. "Hate evil and love good, and establish justice in the gate; it may be that the Lord, the God of hosts, will be gracious to the remnant of Joseph."

but the announcement of what side the church has always been on: as the faithful and flawed vocalization of God's liberating word. Indeed, the place and role of the sub/urban congregation reminds us that the denunciation of injustice must be in word and in deed. It may well need to begin with the church's confession of participation in the creation or support of structures of oppression.[26] The sub/urban church must either do their own in-depth study or support those who undertake the causal analysis of injustice. For instance, why is it that minimum wages are below the poverty level? Who is it that benefits from such structural arrangements? Why is it that so many of the psychologically-wounded appear at our food banks and soup kitchens? What are the causes behind the dearth of affordable and transitional housing? The list seems endless. The church brings to these public conversations a positive stance as well. As it denounces the shortcomings, it can also declare a positive vision of human society as the basis for dreaming the vision of a new city.

For Reflection and Discussion

- What does the word "theology" mean to you? Were there any new insights from the discussion in this chapter? Does your faith community have a local theology? How would you express it?

- Do you have a particular source of news that you trust? Why? Do you get news from multiple sources? What are they?

- If you are part of a faith community, does your community collaborate with any other groups in justice or peace work? What is that experience like? Are there any groups to which you could extend a hand to work on a common issue?

---

26. Guittierez, *A Theology of Liberation*, 267.

Chapter 4

Faith in the City

4.1 BIBLICAL AND THEOLOGICAL VIEWS

God of our streets and cities,
who sets for us agendas that we would not choose,
open our meetings to what really matters.

Let us not confuse correct procedure
with pressing problems,
nor the matter of the media moment
with the problem.
Let us not mistake efficiency with effectiveness,
nor rhetoric with reason.
Teach us to know the difference
and to measure our response.

Where there is boredom, grant us vision;
where there is uncertainty, give us humility;
where there is restlessness, focus;
and in the place of blind rage, excitement.

God of our churches and courts,
who calls us to do the impossible
hear our prayers.[1]

What is the city? In the Christian tradition (growing out of Judaism before it) the city is, at one and the same time, the object of God's historical wrath and of God's promise. Jesus weeps over the city of Jerusalem as did Jeremiah and others before him. The bible notes three primary places where God self-reveals to humanity: mountaintops, deserts, and the city. It may well be that the city is the hardest place to recognize the divine presence and activity. For one thing, there are so many competing options for our attention. For another, sin—however one describes it—seems to gather together in greater concentration there. Third, there are so many hungers present in the city, both our own and others,' real and manufactured. Finally, our own busyness becomes a distraction. I'm not claiming that sub/urban church life is intrinsically harder or more demanding than rural church life. We merely note that, just as the unsuspecting observer may confuse the apparent peacefulness of the countryside with an absence of challenging issues, so too the variety and apparent abundance of resources in the city conceals the size and complexity of human pain and need.

In Hebrew, *city* means an enclosed place. These were initially created for defense. People retreated there, with all they could bring, when the neighborhood was attacked. In scripture, it is the desert that is a dangerous and lonely space. It is the risky spot inhabited by demons and savage animals. To some, cities were places of sanctuary. In the ancient world, there were "sanctuary cities"— if a fleeing criminal made it there, they would be safe from their pursuers. In medieval times, cities were the places where runaway serfs dreamed of establishing a new life, where the newly-wealthy and-literate merchants and craftspeople resisted the traditional demands of power rooted in the land. On the other hand, for those living outside of the city, the relationship was far more negative and parasitic in nature. The city was the place that absorbed the

---

1. Hardy, *Worship in the City*, 134.

food and the labor so badly needed in the hinterland. There are generations of Christian sermons warning of the dangers to body and soul offered by urban wiles and celebrating the spiritual health that rural living afforded.

Today, while metropolitan areas continue to exercise an almost magical appeal for some, for many they are no longer places of refuge. For a growing number they are places of terror. Many of those who flee to the ever-growing cities that burden the planet find a reality vastly different than the dreams they nurtured. Instead of their name in lights and the sort of living seen on television, they experience low-paying jobs, dangerous conditions, unhealthy living spaces, and seemingly endless, uncaring crowds. Many of the cities of the two-thirds world are surrounded by slums, shanty towns, and *favellas,* filled with uncounted numbers of human beings, crammed together without services, economic resources, or even the basic requirements of water and sewage.

Canadian and American cities are really only different in degree. There are increasing numbers of homeless people, begging and sleeping rough, dependent on woefully inadequate social assistance structures. As much as it continues to surprise me, I regularly encounter people who have come to the city with little more than a pair of safety boots and a desire to work, and who are shocked at the difficulty in finding employment. It seems that there are some folks who, in all the challenges of rural life, believe that the city still holds the fulfillment of their dreams.

The bible is an urban book created in an environment dominated by cities. For example, by 2000 BCE Ur (the city of Abraham's origin) had a population of 250,000 (Gen 11:31). Ninevah loomed so large in consciousness that (while archeology does not support such a claim) the author of Jonah talks about three days to walk across it (Jonah 3:3). Babylon, in the time of Nebedcudnezzar (646–582 BCE) had eleven miles of walls and a water and irrigation system (that may have included flush toilets)—an engineering marvel not equaled until the end of the nineteenth century. In the Roman Empire during the early Christian story, Ephesus had street lighting said to be "as bright as day," and Antioch had sixteen miles of colonnaded streets. Of course, nothing equaled Rome, which, in Paul's day, had a population of over 1,000,000 (a figure not equaled until London in the nineteenth century). The city was so congested that wheeled traffic was banned during daylight hours. There were large private mansions and sophisticated apartments, but the poor were jammed into 46,000 wretched tenements that often caught fire, causing horrific loss of life. The following record is given of the public works in Rome in 312–315 BCE:[2]

Table 2: Structures in First-Century Rome

1790 palaces	926 baths	*8 commons
30 parks and gardens	700 public pools	254 bakehouses
290 warehouses	37 gates	36 marble arches
2 circuses	2 amphitheatres	3 theatres
28 libraries	6 obelisks	8 bridges
19 water channels	3785 bronze statues	10,000 carved figures
4 gladiatorial schools	5 nautical spectacles for sea fights	500 fountains fed by 130 reservoirs

We better understand the culture that spawned the bible when we appreciate the power and influence of cities like Rome, Alexandria, Corinth, Babylon, Nineveh, Memphis, and the like. With urban eyes, we can see that much of the content of Paul's letters dealt with ministry in an urban environment. Our pattern, however, is to approach scripture with rural lenses, thinking of the country rather than the city. Thus, in the Psalms, we miss the fact that Mount Zion is not a snow-capped and isolated peak, but the central mountain of Jerusalem.

2. Lithicum, *City of God*, 22.

4.1.1 The City in the Old Testament

In Psalm 42, the psalmist knows where God is—in the tabernacle in the city. The author recalls the joy of pilgrimage to the city. God is in God's city, Jerusalem.

> (vv. 4) These things I remember, as I pour out my soul: how I went with the throng, and led them in procession to the house of God, with glad shouts and songs of thanksgiving, a multitude keeping festival.

> (vv. 11) Why are you cast down, O my soul, and why are you disquieted within me? Hope in God; for I shall again praise him, my help and my God.

Psalm 46 is made up of three segments divided by the refrain: "The LORD of hosts is with us; the God of Jacob is our refuge." Where does God dwell? In the city, in the temple. The divine presence sanctifies the city in the midst of unprecedented chaos: "There is a river whose streams make glad the city of God, the holy habitation of the Most High. God is in the midst of the city; it shall not be moved; God will help it when the morning dawns." (vv. 4–5)

Psalm 48 has been called "the urban dwellers twenty-third Psalm." As such, it is worth quoting at length.

> Great is the LORD and greatly to be praised in the city of our God. His holy mountain, beautiful in elevation, is the joy of all the earth, Mount Zion, in the far north, the city of the great King. Within its citadels God has shown himself a sure defense. Then the kings assembled, they came on together. As soon as they saw it, they were astounded; they were in panic, they took to flight; trembling took hold of them there, pains as of a woman in labor, as when an east wind shatters the ships of Tarshish. As we have heard, so have we seen in the city of the LORD of hosts, in the city of our God, which God establishes forever. Selah We ponder your steadfast love, O God, in the midst of your temple. Your name, O God, like your praise, reaches to the ends of the earth. Your right hand is

filled with victory. Let Mount Zion be glad, let the towns of Judah rejoice because of your judgments. Walk about Zion, go all around it, count its towers, consider well its ramparts; go through its citadels, that you may tell the next generation that this is God, our God forever and ever. He will be our guide forever.

God is to be found primarily within the city (vv. 3). God enters the political process (the threatened assault by foreign kings) and changes it (vv. 4–7). By doing so, God protects this city and (by extension) all the communities of Judah. In its vulnerability, God guards Jerusalem. The psalmist wants to be able to tell subsequent generations—not as a matter of the history of a great city, but as testimony to the presence of God *in that city* (vv. 12–14).

Ezekiel 16:1–14 bears witness, in startlingly unequivocal terms, to the relationship of God with the city of Jerusalem. The metaphor is of an unwanted child, born to an interracial couple, discarded at birth_ and loved only by God (vv. 6–7) that grows up into a lovely young woman with whom God enters into covenant (in explicitly sexual expressions).[3] It is in the context of that covenant that Jerusalem grows rich and prosperous. The city's "abominations" are linked to forgetting the source of its prosperity and believing it could depend upon itself alone.

In a prophecy of consolation, Isaiah 60:1–5, 14–21 calls on the city to "arise and shine, for your light has come, and the glory of the LORD has risen upon you." Despite the darkness and despair that covers the world, God's brightness will be found in Jerusalem and all the people of the earth, from greatest to least, will be drawn to it, bringing with them vast quantities of material wealth as well. The result is a true manifestation of God's shalom in the midst of Jerusalem:

---

3. Your origin and your birth were in the land of the Canaanites; your father was an Amorite, and your mother a Hittite. 4As for your birth, on the day you were born your navel cord was not cut, nor were you washed with water to cleanse you, nor rubbed with salt, nor wrapped in cloths. 5No eye pitied you, to do any of these things for you out of compassion for you; but you were thrown out in the open field, for you were abhorred on the day you were born.

The sun shall no longer be your light by day, nor for brightness shall the moon give light to you by night; but the LORD will be your everlasting light, and your God will be your glory. Your sun shall no more go down, or your moon withdraw itself; for the LORD will be your everlasting light, and your days of mourning shall be ended. Your people shall all be righteous; they shall possess the land forever. They are the shoot that I planted, the work of my hands, so that I might be glorified.

Deuteronomy 6:10–14 forms part of Moses' explanation of the commandments of God to the people of Israel. Within the development of the warning against disobedience, Moses lists a variety of good things that will come to the people when they enter the land being given to them. Note what is listed first in the catalogue: "a land with fine, large cities that you did not build, houses filled with all sorts of goods that you did not fill, hewn cisterns that you did not hew, vineyards and olive groves that you did not plant" (vv. 10–11). It is through passages such as this one, primarily focused on other subjects, that we are reminded of the ways in which cities dominated the perception of those who shaped the canonical form of the biblical text.

Reference has already been made to Jonah and the city of Nineveh. The scholarly assumption is that the book was written in response to a form of hyper-religious-nationalism that insisted that the care and concern of God was only for the people of Israel. The reluctant prophet is such an exemplar of that view that, in the service of God, he is prepared to resist the command of God. That there were good, concrete reasons for a Hebrew prophet to despise the powerful and militarily aggressive Ninevites, and all they stood for, only heightens the irony of the text. In a reversal of Abraham haggling with God for the souls of Sodom and Gomorrah (Gen 18:23), the divine presses Jonah to be concerned for "the great city," not only the people but the domestic livestock as well.[4]

---

4. "And should I not be concerned about Nineveh, that great city, in which there are more than a hundred and twenty thousand persons who do not know their right hand from their left, and also many animals?"(4:11)

When we turn to Nineveh, we begin to bring into focus the problems with the "city" (generally cast as Jerusalem). Isaiah 58:3–7 locates the symptom of the problem in the peoples' sense that God is no longer attentive to their worship. Speaking for the people the prophet asks: "Why do we fast, but you do not see? Why humble ourselves, but you do not notice?" (vv. 3). The response is that the people fail to express the faith they assert in worship through the realities of daily living. The problems identified are systemic in nature: economic, political, and social irresponsibility toward the poor.[5]

Jeremiah takes these surface problems and traces them to idolatry. This idolatry, the breaking of the covenant with Yahweh, manifests itself in self-indulgence, economic injustice, exploitation, and oppression of the less powerful. These are all the actions of people who have given themselves over to serve other gods: money, power, prestige, and the commitment to their own group.[6] The forecast result of such betrayal will serve as a warning to all against the path taken by Jerusalem.

---

5. "Look, you serve your own interest on your fast day, and oppress all your workers. Look, you fast only to quarrel and to fight and to strike with a wicked fist. Such fasting as you do today will not make your voice heard on high. Is such the fast that I choose, a day to humble oneself? Is it to bow down the head like a bulrush, and to lie in sackcloth and ashes? Will you call this a fast, a day acceptable to the LORD? Is not this the fast that I choose: to loose the bonds of injustice, to undo the thongs of the yoke, to let the oppressed go free, and to break every yoke? Is it not to share your bread with the hungry, and bring the homeless poor into your house; when you see the naked, to cover them, and not to hide yourself from your own kin?" (58:3–7). See also Isa 59:12–14.

6. You shall say: Hear the word of the LORD, O kings of Judah and inhabitants of Jerusalem. Thus says the LORD of hosts, the God of Israel: I am going to bring such disaster upon this place that the ears of everyone who hears of it will tingle. Because the people have forsaken me, and have profaned this place by making offerings in it to other gods whom neither they nor their ancestors nor the kings of Judah have known, and because they have filled this place with the blood of the innocent, and gone on building the high places of Baal to burn their children in the fire as burnt offerings to Baal, which I did not command or decree, nor did it enter my mind;" Jer 19:3–5.

And many nations will pass by this city, and all of them will say one to another, "Why has the LORD dealt in this way with that great city?" And they will answer, "Because they abandoned the covenant of the LORD their God, and worshiped other gods and served them," (Jer 22:8–9).

Ezekiel develops the theme yet a further step. In his complaints against the city (chapter 22), we find that the issue is not *only* that great evil is being committed, but that the city itself has become corrupt. It is infamous, detestable, and murderous, suffering the scorn of the nations (vv. 4). The corruption is found in political processes as the leaders pillage everyone for their own gain (vv. 6–7, 25); its religious practices are debased (vv. 8–9, 26); and its economic practices are focused entirely on the expansion of dishonest gain (vv. 12–13, 27).

The prophet wants the listener to understand the extent of the corruption in the city, perhaps to forestall the suggestion that it is all about a "few bad apples." No, in this city the princes have exchanged their caring and guiding task for the guise of a roaring lion, feeding on anything it touches and oppressing those less powerful. The economic and business elites, in the course of the legitimate practice of their trades, have become wolves, taking not only legitimate profits but whatever they can acquire through bribery, self-interest, and extortion. The religious leaders are fully participant in this horror as well, doing violence to Yahweh's word, profaning holy things, denying the Sabbath. Worst of all, those who should be calling the leadership to account, the prophets, have been co-opted by the system: "Its prophets have smeared whitewash on their behalf, seeing false visions and divining lies for them, saying, 'Thus says the Lord GOD,' when the LORD has not spoken." (vv. 27–28). Finally, this has corrupted the entire people (vv. 8–11, 29).

4.1.2 Case Studies

Given the historical record—Christianity's birth as a primarily urban movement—there is a striking absence of awareness of a sub/urban reality in much contemporary reflection. Very few of the huge number of sermons preached on the Pauline epistles note that they are written to city people. From the new testament record it appears that, once the faith in Jesus of Nazareth as Messiah had migrated from Palestine to the wider Roman Empire, rural areas such as Galilee were largely ignored. On the other hand, after Paul and Augustine, almost no major theological writer worked in an urban setting until the eighteenth century. Calvin's Geneva, although considered a city, numbered approximately 16,000 souls—in other words, a moderate sized-town by twenty-first century standards. So, what does the bible say about the city? In what follows I want to look at nine cities (the seven in the Revelation, plus Jerusalem, and Babylon).

The churches of the Revelation are of particular interest to sub/urban congregations because the analysis focuses on characteristics such as nurture and support; the relationship of membership to attendance; the sharing of time, treasure and talents; and the ministries maintained.[7] The constant emphasis on increased numbers (membership, attendance, revenue, etc.) that so often drives conversation about the "success or failure" of ministries is problematic in its application to sub/urban churches where different factors come into play.

Revelation is notoriously difficult to interpret. It has been hijacked by particular expressions of the tradition as a series of predictions for the future. Different groups engage in increasingly fevered attempts to relate words and phrases to events in daily news, all the while endeavoring to determine that these are the "end times." Those who engage in such practices are not at all deterred by the fact that, repeatedly in the last two millennia, faithful Christians have looked at their context and believed that theirs was the time. Nor do they seem at all troubled by Jesus' warning

---

7. Lithicum, *City of God*, 297.

not to be absorbed in plotting the day or the hour, or affected by his own willingness to remain ignorant of the subject.

For our purposes, it is enough to recognize that the author of the book, John the Seer, was writing to his contemporaries at a time when the infant congregations of the faithful were facing a variety of challenges. Some of these were manifested from outside while others addressed were internal in origin. To these urban churches, John writes:

> I, John, your brother who share with you in Jesus the persecution and the kingdom and the patient endurance, was on the island called Patmos because of the word of God and the testimony of Jesus. I was in the spirit on the Lord's day, and I heard behind me a loud voice like a trumpet saying, "Write in a book what you see and send it to the seven churches, to Ephesus, to Smyrna, to Pergamum, to Thyatira, to Sardis, to Philadelphia, and to Laodicea." (1:9–11)

Here we find that the author was claiming a relationship of faith and struggle with those to whom he writes. The recipients are the *angels* of the seven churches in seven pivotal cities. Any congregation has a personality or a quality. Often visitors will refer to a church as "warm" or "friendly" or "aloof." Sometimes we can point to particular manifestations of the personality in specific actions. More often it is just a sense or a feeling. One approach that is useful in sub/urban ministry (in concert with others) is to be aware of the principalities and powers at work in the city.[8] In each letter we find an analysis of the context: history, commerce, religious, and political. The underlying and unspoken question seems to be: "How have you reacted to the city around you as you sought to be in ministry to it?" After that analysis come words meant to redirect

---

8. In understanding contemporary explorations of the biblical concept of "principalities and powers," the series by Walter Wink is an invaluable resource. *Engaging the Powers: Discernment and Resistance in a World of Domination* (1982); *Naming the Powers: The Language of Power in the New Testament* (1984); and *Unmasking the Powers: The Invisible Forces that Determine Human Existence* (1986).

and encourage that urban ministry. That will serve to shape our first seven case studies.

We should briefly note that each of the letters contains an introduction and a conclusion that are specific to that congregation. The former declares certain qualities of the Spirit/Christ and the latter are promises of action for good or ill. These verses are particularly steeped in the themes and metaphors of apocalyptic Jewish and early Christian thought and, while interesting, need not delay our study. They serve as a reminder, however, of the degree to which the author of the Revelation was intimately aware of both the context and ministry of each congregation.

Study 1

Name: Ephesus

Text: Revelation 2:1–7

To the angel of the church in Ephesus write: These are the words of him who holds the seven stars in his right hand, who walks among the seven golden lamp stands: "I know your works, your toil and your patient endurance. I know that you cannot tolerate evildoers; you have tested those who claim to be apostles but are not, and have found them to be false. I also know that you are enduring patiently and bearing up for the sake of my name, and that you have not grown weary. But I have this against you, that you have abandoned the love you had at first. Remember then from what you have fallen; repent, and do the works you did at first. If not, I will come to you and remove your lampstand from its place, unless you repent. Yet this is to your credit: you hate the works of the Nicolaitans, which I also hate. Let anyone who has an ear listen to what the Spirit is saying to the churches. To everyone who conquers, I will give permission to eat from the tree of life that is in the paradise of God.

Faith in the City

Context

Ephesus was Asia's greatest and most strategic city. Its magnificent harbour formed the nexus of a series of road networks dating from pre-Roman times. It had the unusual status of being a free city (no Roman troops were quartered there). It was also a place where legal cases were tried. The inscription of the public buildings reflected that status: *Lumen Asiae* (the Light of Asia). The population was a gathering of Greek and Asian tribes and Ephesus was often cited as a premier exemplar of the truly Roman city.

Church

In Ephesus, Christianity was in competition with a variety of rich religious traditions. The city was a center for the worship of Artemis/Diana, a very powerful force in the eastern Roman empire. John is an informed commentator. Note the compliments he pays the congregation. They have been tested and borne up under pressure from outside. He recognizes: "your toil and your patient endurance," and "you are enduring patiently and bearing up for the sake of my name, and that you have not grown weary." It is more than simple stubbornness. The congregation has been open to outside ideas but not swept away by every fad: "you have tested those who . . ." come claiming to represent the gospel. Most significantly, they have resisted the Nicolaitans.

In reading these letters, it is helpful to recall a couple of realities. The first is that our contemporary separation of religion, politics, and business into different *spheres* of life would make no sense in the first century. They were all tied together. For instance, in most cities, trade and commerce was controlled by the various guilds. Each would have its own temple and its own rituals for elected gods. Meetings and gatherings of the guild members would take place in the context of rituals of worship and feasts in honor of the god. Those unwilling to take part in the "spiritual" aspects of the guild would find their commercial activities greatly restricted or rendered impossible. A second reality is that in these early years of the Christian story there were many different versions of the faith, each claiming to be the truth. The Nicolaitans were followers of a branch that sought to minimize the differences between Christians and the Roman society around them. By taking Paul's arguments to an extreme, they reasoned that, since the Jewish law no longer applied to followers of Christ, then there should be no restrictions on his followers' morality and behavior, especially when those restrictions would differentiate them from the social context.

Despite the allure of the Nicolaitans' arguments, which were backed up by the challenges Christians encountered in the marketplace, the congregation has remained firm in the faith. However, under that pressure they have grown cold and hard. They are afraid of newcomers—and perhaps a little afraid of one another. Instead of encountering the spiritual and intellectual challenges posed by their context, they have opted for a brittle purity of belief and practice. The cost has been the death of warmth and joy. The prescription of the Spirit is a return to the character of an earlier time. Return to that time when you first started on this journey: treat one another differently; spend time in worshipping God not just defending God; spend less energy preserving the faith and more time enjoying it; and, heal the breaches that your emphasis on spiritual purity have caused. The alternative is a doctrinally pure, emotionally loveless, increasingly joyless and judgmental community; in other words, something that is not Christian, despite its efforts to be such.

Observations

It is not difficult to find sub/urban congregations struggling with the "Ephesian-disease."[9]

In response to societal changes they have become fortresses, enclaves of purity in what is seen as a sea of evil. In their favor, they

---

9. In each case, I intend to explore the challenges of the particular congregation realizing that the reverse appears in another letter. John is amazingly comprehensive in his analyses of urban ministry.

have not succumbed to the popular notions that Christian faith is a purely private matter that has no impact in business or political practices. They have preserved the, often-misplaced, awareness that a Christian is something more than a good citizen with the occasional Sunday morning appointment. Such congregations may provide an intense feeling of belonging for those inside but are remarkably resistant to newcomers. Of course, every failure of a newcomer to graft onto the congregation simply reinforces the purity that the congregation believes is their defining quality.[10] The appeal of such a community of diamond-hard clarity in the midst of postmodern searching can be significant. In contrast to the (perceived) mainline church failure to stand for anything, these congregations gain followers by standing for something. The "refugees" and wounded from such experiences often appear in sub/urban churches. Those congregations must be particularly sensitive to the ways in which those newcomers have been taught to understand basic Christian vocabulary. In their zeal for purity, these congregations have shut out any possible interaction with the thought and faith of the world around them. They avoid infection but also miss the nourishment that comes from open dialogue.

Study 2

Name: Smyrna

Text: Revelation 2:8–11

And to the angel of the church in Smyrna write: These are the words of the first and the last, who was dead and came to life: "I know your affliction and your poverty, even though you are rich. I know the slander on the part of those who say that they are Jews and are not, but are

---

10. In workshops, I sometimes ask participants to draw a picture of the view of their congregation in its community. The most vivid example I recall was the woman who drew a medieval castle, surrounded by a moat populated by what seemed to be sharks. The drawbridge was up and everything around was in shadow.

a synagogue of Satan. Do not fear what you are about to suffer. Beware, the devil is about to throw some of you into prison so that you may be tested, and for ten days *you will* have affliction. Be faithful until death, and I will give you the crown of life. Let anyone who has an ear listen to what the Spirit is saying to the churches. Whoever conquers will not be harmed by the second death.

Context

"The fairest of the cities of Iona" (according to the Roman writer Lucian), Smyrna was a great trading community. It was graced by a constant west wind that cooled the city, and a large and well-protected harbour at its center. Unlike the majority of cities in the world (ancient and modern), this was a planned area, with broad streets and astonishing architecture. It also had a large, powerful and vocal Jewish community.[11] Its most famous Christian was Polycarp, who was burned at the stake in 155 CE. Refusing to sacrifice to Caesar, Polycarp is quoted as saying: "Eighty and six years have I served him, and he has done me no wrong. How can I blaspheme my King, who saved me?"[12]

Church

This letter was written to a church under persecution, its members suffering affliction, poverty, and imprisonment. It seems there was an intentional program on the part of some or all community leaders to end this church. The text is largely focused on the Jewish colonists in Smyrna. In reading works that come from the Johannine literature (gospel, letters, and Revelation) contemporary readers need to hold in mind the evolution of Christianity from a group of faithful Jews, who believed in Jesus of Nazareth

---

11. http://en.wikipedia.org/wiki/Smyrna. Meinardus, Otto F. A. *St. John of Patmos and the Seven Churches of the Apocalypse.* Athens: Aristide D Caratzas Pub, 1979.

12. http://www.polycarp.net/.

as the Messiah, to a mixed community of Jews and Gentiles who were no longer comfortable or welcome within Judaism. As a result, in the time of John, Jewish-Christian relations were bitter in that way that seems reserved to sibling quarrels and civil wars. The Jews, who had achieved certain unique rights and privileges in the empire, wanted to clearly separate themselves from this upstart group. They may well have engaged in slander against the Christians, raising fears about them and urging the state to persecute them. Since the Christians did that, there is no reason to suppose that the Jews refrained.

Observations

The letter is refreshingly straightforward and down to earth. No sign here of: "Well, just have enough faith and everything will go your way." The focus is kept resolutely on the church's spiritual wealth and the dangers of following Christ as if the two are inextricably linked. Testing will come, some of them will go to jail, and for some it may involve death. It required no particular gift of prophecy to reach that conclusion in the context of religious persecution. They are enjoined to fix their attention on Jesus, the one who could be killed but could not be stopped. The Risen One has exposed the lie of the persecuting powers: they threw everything they could at him (including mockery, shame, torture, and death) and he was victorious by God's grace. That promise is held out to this struggling remnant as well.

Contemporary sub/urban churches generally face pressures of a less direct kind than our ancestors in Smyrna. There may not be groups calling for destruction, although some of the tactics of the rising religious right in North America (particularly around hot button issues like homosexuality and family structure) may be experienced as destructive.[13] On the other hand, we certainly

---

13. Roy Oswald and Loren Mead of the Alban Institute maintain that the next great challenge to the churches might be the revocation of their tax-exempt status. This possibility is sometimes raised in Canada in terms of removing municipal property tax exemption.

do not dwell in a prejudice-free society. Having been, in our time, both victim and perpetrator of prejudice, perhaps we are placed to share in the defense of those who are blameless yet are blamed for the actions of those who bear the same name. If we've ever been tarred with the brush of "those Christians," then we know how difficult and unjust that is to bear. As I read this letter again I could not help but think of the group that some voices might label the "mosque of Satan," namely radical Islam, and the attempt of some political leaders to grasp power through the fostering of hatred and suspicion of all Muslims. The sub/urban church, living in the midst of the multicultural reality that is the modern city, is placed to use its position and resources to overcome fear, distrust, and ignorance by providing safe venues for growing knowledge and increased exposure to the truth.

In the face of persecution, the Smyrnan Christians are urged to keep the focus on Jesus Christ. The letter to Smyrna serves as a reminder to urban Christians in the first world that, while we may not be suffering direct persecution, we need to take seriously our connections with sisters and brothers in the faith who are. In my trips to the two-thirds world, I have been forcibly reminded of how powerful North American citizens are. We can lobby government and write to newspapers without fear of the knock at the door in the night that precedes disappearance. Amnesty International is one example of an organization that, through the power of individuals willing to write to dictatorial regimes, has secured some measure of amelioration in abysmal human rights situations.

Study 3

Name: Pergamum

Text: Revelation 2:12–17

And to the angel of the church in Pergamum write: These are the words of him who has the sharp two-edged sword: "I know where you are living, where Satan's throne is. Yet you are holding fast to my name, and you did not deny your faith in me even in the days of Antipas my witness, my faithful one, who was killed among you, where Satan lives. But I have a few things against you: you have some there who hold to the teaching of Balaam, who taught Balak to put a stumbling block before the people of Israel, so that they would eat food sacrificed to idols and practice fornication. So you also have some who hold to the teaching of the Nicolaitans. Repent then. If not, I will come to you soon and make war against them with the sword of my mouth. Let anyone who has an ear listen to what the Spirit is saying to the churches. To everyone who conquers I will give some of the hidden manna, and I will give a white stone, and on the white stone is written a new name that no one knows except the one who receives it.

Context

The political capital of Asia Minor (modern Turkey) for nearly 400 years, Pergamum had a marvelous physical location. It held the finest library in Asia (some 200,000 parchment scrolls)—indeed, parchment was invented there. It was a center for the worship of three gods: Zeus, Athena and Asclepius. The latter was the god of healing whose temples were amongst the first hospitals.

The city was the administrative capital of Roman Asia. It was this that led to the comment about the city where "Satan has his throne." For most people in the ancient world, the existence of multiple gods was simply common sense. Indeed, Jews and Christians were labeled "atheists" for their insistence that there was only one God. If they relocated, the most common pattern was for people to simply add new gods to their existing personal pantheon. Thus, while certain gods had large followings across the empire, most gods were more localized in their groups of devotees. The Roman Empire was remarkably tolerant in matters of religious conviction. You could believe or not believe as you chose, as long as you participated in the state religion. The cult of the Divine Emperor was the glue that held these disparate convictions together. It was neither a particularly convincing nor moving belief. Rather, it was a common veneer over the spiritual life of the empire. It involved, at a variety of semi-regular times, the placing of a pinch of incense on a brazier and saying, "Caesar is Lord." This action also served as a test of loyalty to the empire.

The Jews were virtually unique in being excused from this requirement. As the differences between Christians and Jews became more marked, the former was increasingly required to show their loyalty through the observance of the emperor's divinity. Failure to comply was taken as evidence of treason.[14] Pergamum, as a regional political center, was also the center for emperor worship in Asia Minor, and for the early Christians, nothing was more Satanic than substituting Caesar for Christ. This became the focus for very real civil conflict for a couple of centuries.

Church

First Church Pergamum was truly caught in a cleft stick. It ministered in one of the period's most difficult locations for Christian faith. Due to the proximity of senior government officials, lesser bureaucrats were particularly zealous in enforcing all the laws. Practices that might have been winked at in more remote locations felt the full burden of legal displeasure. Despite that, the members of this congregation have held true to their faith. Even in the face of martyrdom,[15] they have remained loyal. However, that loyalty is tainted by the toleration of certain deviant groups. Nicolaitans we have already encountered—they were economic and social

---

14. It is rarely understood that for most regimes down through the 1700s, persecution was not fueled by religious reasons, but for causes of civil order. In most societies, it was not conceivable that people could have different spiritual convictions and exist side-by-side. This was particularly true in legal and state matters where differing faith commitments raised the specter of unreliable oaths and other aberrations. If you and I believe in different gods, how can you trust any oaths that I undertake? This, of course, did not prevent victims of persecution from perceiving a religious basis for their suffering.

15. The Antipas in this reading is otherwise unknown.

accommodationists. Balaamites were probably political conformists, arguing that participation in the Emperor cult could not really harm Christians whose deepest loyalties lay elsewhere. The congregation is urged to deal with these deviancies. Those who are faithful are promised two tokens. Hidden manna probably refers to the feeding of the Israelites in the desert and the bread of the Eucharist. The white stone may refer to a common pagan practice of carrying around a stone inscribed with the name of the god as a good luck amulet. White, of course, is the colour of purity, and the potency of hidden or secret names was widely accepted in the ancient world.

Observations

How should the sub/urban church respond to pressures to conform? Where do we draw the line on behaviors, or is the language of "line drawing" even appropriate or helpful? There are certainly Christian communities which make non-participation in some socially accepted practices a hallmark of faithfulness. This would appear easier to do in a community that, in every way practical, lives a separated existence from the surrounding society. At the other extreme, there are high profile Christian groups that have bought into the values of the society to the extent that they teach it as God's will that the faithful possess all of the consumerist marks of success. Churches also vary widely in the degree to which they endorse specific government policies at any given time. Those who oppose in the name of the gospel are often told that the church should stay out of politics. Apparently, supporting government isn't political but opposition is.

Sub/urban ministries are in constant interaction with the surrounding consumer culture. Some of their long-time members may even recall the era when church participation was considered good for business. Unlike urban missions which focus on those who are victims and/or marginalized in the current society, sub/urban ministries may have leaders of business, politics, professions, and academia amongst their numbers. Later in this discussion, I want to explore the idea that the presence of such folks affords the church a great resource in seeking justice and truth in the city's life. So, how can the church minister to—and with—these folks for whom (my experience suggests) the moral and "Christian" exercise of their authority often bulks large in their list of concerns? Several possibilities suggest themselves:

a. A clear congregational theology of stewardship is essential. Through open conversation and study, determine what guidance the bible gives twenty-first century followers of Jesus in the use of what they steward. Note that while the advice given to the rich young man to sell all that he has may apply to some, Jesus was far more nuanced in his spiritual counsel than we often are.[16] The urban congregation can model such stewardship in its relationships with community groups as well as helping individual members and families recognize and own healthy, faithful, and personal standards.

b. The Nicolaitans were loathed because the practices that they advanced would have involved Christians engaging in the worship of other gods. Most of those gods were represented by idols of stone, wood, or metal. Because they do not worship in the presence of such statues, members of the sub/urban congregation may miss the danger of idolatry in their personal faith. The material of which an idol is made is irrelevant; the significance is found in the place it holds in the individual's hierarchy of values. Sub/urban ministries need to aid their members in attending to idolatry in their lives. Sub/urban churches also need to be attentive to the degree to which they adopt attitudes and practices of the society and incorporate them into congregational life.

c. Many congregations will be very receptive to instruction about living the faith in the workplace. There are numerous print and online resources (from a mainline perspective) that are helpful in this inquiry. A study or sermon series on such a subject should provide both the theory and practice of what it

---

16. Mark 10:17–26 and the parallel, Luke 18:18–30.

means to be a follower of Jesus in the world. If it is to be helpful, then it is important to develop such a series in conversation with those who know what such a context truly entails.

d. Most sub/urban church members see themselves as loyal citizens, and if that was all the Balaamites were promoting then it should cause no problem. However, from a Christian perspective, by advocating participation in the emperor cult they were (intentionally or not) promoting a different highest loyalty for the followers. In any context there will be debate about what "loyalty" entails. By the same token, the tradition of various types of civil disobedience for the purpose of drawing to the attention of those in authority a higher good is well-established. What is clear is that any claim to "neutrality" is a sham: it merely supports the status quo.[17] If the existing situation is unjust then silence renders the church complicit in injustice. What can the sub/urban church do?

  i. Provide and promote alternative news sources;
  ii. Cooperate with justice-seeking social groups;[18]
  iii. Engage in sermon, study, and speakers' series;[19]
  iv. Form coalitions with other religious groups

17. Recall our discussion of Ezekiel 22 above.

18. Here it is important to be cognizant of the different commitments of church and other groups. Recently, one congregation was asked to be the "sanctuary place" during protests against a major economic summit. During the conversations, it became clear that the organizers of the event, while not condoning violence, were not prepared to explicitly renounce its use by protestors. Church leaders were faced with the possibility of perpetrators of violence seeking sanctuary in our church. While not for a moment condoning the violence often employed by security forces, that refusal to renounce violent protest made participation *in that fashion*, impossible. The congregation did have a presence at the protest. This example is offered, not as a prescription, but to demonstrate the importance of the fullest possible clarity in such alliances.

19. Reports of IRS activities in the United States and the activities of Revenue Canada (Canada's regulator of charitable status) suggest that congregations going this route may need to consider those implications of such actions. Again, the suggestion is not that we avoid acts of faithfulness but that we be as aware as possible of their ramifications. The brave community is not one that feels no fear; it is the one that sees the reasons to fear and still responds to a higher calling.

(especially non-Christian ones) to address issues;
v. Formulate broad resolutions to governments;
vi. Equip and encourage members to make their own representations to authorities, either publicly or in private;
vii. Have a visible presence at public gatherings on the subject;
viii. Use national and international church networks to explore and advance alternative suggestions;
ix. Foster and provide a safe environment where differing viewpoints can be explored in an atmosphere of robust Christian love.

Study 4

Name: Thyatira

Text: Revelation 2:18–29

And to the angel of the church in Thyatira write: These are the words of the Son of God, who has eyes like a flame of fire, and whose feet are like burnished bronze: "I know your works—your love, faith, service, and patient endurance. I know that your last works are greater than the first. But I have this against you: you tolerate that woman Jezebel, who calls herself a prophet and is teaching and beguiling my servants to practice fornication and to eat food sacrificed to idols. I gave her time to repent, but she refuses to repent of her fornication. Beware, I am throwing her on a bed, and those who commit adultery with her I am throwing into great distress, unless they repent of her doings; and I will strike her children dead. And all the churches will know that I am the one who searches minds and hearts, and I will give to each of you as your works deserve. But to the rest of you in Thyatira, who do not hold this teaching, who have not learned what some call 'the deep things of Satan,' to you I say, I do not lay on you any other burden; only hold fast to what you have until I come. To everyone who conquers and continues to do my works to the end, I will give authority over the nations; to rule them with an iron rod, as when clay pots are shattered—even as I also received authority from my Father. To the one who conquers I will also give the morning star. Let anyone who has an ear listen to what the Spirit is saying to the churches.

Context

The least important of the seven cities, Thyatira is consequently the one we know the least about. It was located in a valley that led to Pergamum and may have had its origins simply as a defense of its larger sister. However, since the location was largely indefensible the only act would be to slow the attackers down. Because of its location on a major road, it was a commercial center with a large number of guilds devoted to various crafts including wool, leather, linen, bronze, outer garments, material dying, pottery, and baked goods. As we noted earlier, these guilds were a combination of trade union and trade association, social clubs, and special interest lobby groups, each with its own patron god and religious aspects. Many contemporary authors refer to the immoral activities that went on at the common meals of the guilds. Membership in a guild was central to success in any trade.

While in Philippi, Paul and Silas stayed with a woman named Lydia from Thyatira, who continued an important role in that church after the missionaries' release from prison and departure from the city (Acts 16:14).

Church

The church in this city was vibrant and prosperous. If we asked someone on the street they could tell us that it was well-known for its good deeds and service to the needy. It was populated with generous members and had a quality of life that was attractive to all. One of the signs of the love of God is a willingness to serve others.

Such faith is often contagious and causes the congregation to grow, not through any evangelistic plan, but simply by the attractiveness of faithful living. We might even suppose that the current state of that congregation was far better than when it began. The letter commences by noting these commendable qualities.

However, there is more to be said to the angel of this church. Apparently, there was a popular and powerful woman in the congregation who was urging greater participation in the life of the city—including the guilds. She advocated what was necessary to promote business. But this compromises the very thing that sets the church off from the city. There is a warning of a coming punishment, the business failure and destruction of those who compromised because they had rejected the very grounds on which the church's popularity had risen. They needed to get their ideas straight and return to following Christ. Nothing more and nothing less. There are times when we make Christianity more outwardly demanding than it really is or create long lists of things that we should do. Some promote special knowledge or special rituals. In fact, the formula remains as simple and as demanding as it always was: love for God, neighbor, and self. If the good folks at Thyatira could hold to that, then the writer would be well pleased with them.

Observations

Each of the angels who received a letter represented a church that was in a unique situation with specific challenges to faithfulness. In Thyatira the issue was the compromise represented by guild membership. The sexual activities that were featured as part of guild life constituted but one part of the problem, albeit a very obvious one. For many students, the obvious sexual references in this letter have served as a jumping off point for an attack on perceived failings in contemporary morality. As a result, many who are outside the church perceive it as being absolutely absorbed with sex, to the exclusion of any other concern. Sex, the sex trade, and other forms of sexual impropriety are a feature of sub/urban reality that the church must be aware of. We must also avoid the appearance or conviction that sexual expression, in and of itself, is what Christianity is all about. An undergraduate is reported to have asked a campus chaplain why Christians were so hung up on sex. He answered, "If we can get you to listen to God on the little things, then maybe we can move on to important things, like money and time."[20]

Because the sub/urban church is in the center of a highly sexualized social milieu, issues of human sexuality cannot be ignored in the teaching about a faithful lifestyle. But it is just that, a lifestyle. Increasingly sub/urban churches are recognizing the need to form disciples rather than merely members. Not only can we no longer count on newcomers to know anything of the basics of the faith, by the same token we need to realize that they (as well as long-timers) may need direct, concentrated small group opportunity to develop a fully rounded Christian life. Is there any role for the church (for your church) in disciplining members whose practices are outside a certain moral standard? If Christian faith never confronts us with difficult challenges and choices, how real is it?

Many sub/urban clergy read of the activities of better-known clergy and congregations in large centers and think that that is where the action is for witnessing justice. As a consequence, activist sub/urban churches may overlook opportunities for faithful witness because they believe their cities to be small, unimportant, or far from the seats of power. The letter to Thyatira reminds us that the risen one has a concern for every community of faith, regardless of its setting, and that there are more than enough issues of justice for all to address.

In this letter, Jezebel is referred to as a prophetess. Let's be clear, the issue is not one of gender. The issue was her teaching that it was okay to go along with the pressures of making a living and God would understand and overlook such choices. Her philosophy was what you often hear today: "Business is business."

---

20. I recall the comment as being attributed to William Willimon when he was Dean of the Chapel at Duke University but have been unable to locate a source for it. Even apocryphally it serves as a wonderful reminder.

If business practices collide with your Christian principles, then your principles have to go—because you have to make a living. Does that argument sound familiar? The Nicolaitans are alive and well in the twenty-first century. The sub/urban church must be constantly aware of the balance between openness of welcome and the erasing of all distinctives. For instance, at what point does the exploration of issues and convictions lead us to the point of losing our Christian identity? When do we say to someone who holds a particular viewpoint: "We respect your right to believe that, but we need you to stop proclaiming it in this community as if it were acceptable Christian teaching?" Of course, to accomplish that, we need to understand the limits of faith that our community subscribes to.

Study 5

Name: Sardis

Text: Revelation 3:1–6

> And to the angel of the church in Sardis write: These are the words of him who has the seven spirits of God and the seven stars: "I know your works; you have a name of being alive, but you are dead. Wake up, and strengthen what remains and is on the point of death, for I have not found your works perfect in the sight of my God. Remember then what you received and heard; obey it, and repent. If you do not wake up, I will come like a thief, and you will not know at what hour I will come to you. Yet you have still a few persons in Sardis who have not soiled their clothes; they will walk with me, dressed in white, for they are worthy. If you conquer, you will be clothed like them in white robes, and I will not blot your name out of the book of life; I will confess your name before my Father and before his angels. Let anyone who has an ear listen to what the Spirit is saying to the churches.

Context

The city of Sardis was a stark contrast of former splendor and present decay. It was one of the great cities of Asia Minor from the seventh century BCE until the time of the Eastern Roman Empire. Legend had it that, in the sixth century, it was ruled by Croesus, whose name is a byword for uncountable wealth. It was built on a mountain spur about 1,500 feet above the valley floor and was deemed virtually impregnable. In the several efforts to capture it through the centuries, the two times it fell were due to stealth and the carelessness of the defenders. Sardis was an important center for the manufacturing and dyeing of delicate woolen products.

Church

The Spirit has nothing good to say about the Sardinian church. The letter begins with the observation that a reputation for activity is belied by a reality of somnolence. Indeed, it is worse: what is reputed to be alive is dead. It may well be that worship in this church was liturgically correct, the music was technically proficient, perhaps the participants considered themselves to be believers, and all the boxes in annual denominational report forms were completed, but in truth it was unresponsive and lethargic. It faced none of the overwhelming problems of the other churches—neither persecution nor heresy. It may be that no one there believed enough to cause controversy or to be targeted.

Where was the hope for this congregation? It needed to remember its vitality. It needed to shift from the self-absorbed focus of polite conventionality to the risk of discipleship. At one point, it had been a lively community, full of people exploring their relationship to God and the implications for daily living. The church needed to go back to obeying the commands of Christ—perhaps even to the point of bringing persecution on their own heads. Their challenge was to push back against a passive and non-demanding form of faith. It seems the key to that future was to be found in a small group. Somewhere in that mass of stultifying formalism there was the nucleus of discipleship. Chances are that the more refined fellow-members looked down on this cadre. They were always writing letters, raising issues, or talking about the latest book they'd read by a controversial Christian author. This was the group that held the future in their hands.

Observations

One of the great challenges to sub/urban congregations is "Sardis disease." It is one of the common features of the cognitive dissonance we explored earlier. Many sub/urban congregations live on their past glory. You can see it in the pictures on the wall—lots from back then, none from right now. They pride themselves on ministries they once began but wouldn't dream of starting something new. No one in the "Young Couples Club" has been married for fewer than twenty-five years. The stories are all of the great days when there were hundreds of children in the Sunday School and people lined up to get in for worship. Now the great concern is to keep the church going just as it was. Any plan for the future is summarized in the hoped-for return of an undefined multitude.

It is fitting and faithful that some sub/urban mainline churches die. I say that without rancour or joy. Some of them were products of the Christendom-era when social convention and legal structures supported church attendance. Such days are both unwelcome and unlikely to return. In those days, denominations erected hundreds of churches to meet the demand of an overwhelmingly Christian population. In the years since, not only has church participation fallen on hard times, multiracial and multicultural growth have irrevocably changed the population of the city. Even if, by some fluke, churches were to return to the same proportion of the population attending worship, the size of the potential group has shrunk. Meanwhile, unspeakable quantities of every kind of resource are being poured into keeping congregations alive that are no more animate than was that in Sardis. At least some people are honest. At more than one church event I've been told by senior congregation members: "As long as it stays open until my funeral I don't care what happens then." The tragedy is that, until that occurs, especially in denominations without structures that can force the issue, resources will be squandered in horrific fashion and those Sardis-like congregations that want to come back to their first love may not find sufficient support for the journey.

In the Sardis-congregations in cities across North America there are small groups who—for whatever reasons of love, loyalty, or inertia—have not abandoned themselves to the dull routine, the spiritless worship, and the repetitive shuffling of the chairs. They yearn for something more, something deeper, and something with greater life. In short, they dream of being a church of Jesus Christ. Since no life-altering decision ever came from a committee, it falls to those people, whoever they are and whatever roles they fill, to come together and find one thing that animates them. Then they need to start doing it. "It" could be an outreach project, music group, study circle, prayer chain, or any one of a number of things. Perhaps there is something in the congregation's history that can be spiritually revived, or a current program that would truly benefit from an injection of enthusiasm. Remember, the seeds of the future for the church in Sardis were found in its past enthusiasms and commitments. The point is not to get it right straight off. There is much truth in the wisdom that says when we're stuck we need to do anything and make course corrections later. Eventually, if done prayerfully and faithfully, any activity which generates passion will attract others.

The other grim reality of the modern Sardis-congregation is the refusal to countenance risk. In every form of business risk is a condition of growth.[21] If we refuse to take risks and continue with what is secure and safe we may have the appearance of life but be dead. In the sciences, there is no such thing as a failed experiment. It may not have achieved the results anticipated but that teaches

---

21. It is important to remember that "growth" is not restricted to revenue or attendance. Loren Mead speaks of growth in terms of participants, service, knowledge, spiritual maturity and finances in his book, *More Than Numbers: The Way That Churches Grow*.

the researcher something. Many congregations I know are gripped by the apparent conviction that any error is terminal. They have a culture that assiduously slaps down anyone who tries to do things in a new way because "it might not work." Unless such a tradition is confronted and shown to be the destructive force that it is, the Sardis church will be unable to return to its former liveliness.

Study 6

Name: Philadelphia

Text: Revelation 3:7–13

> And to the angel of the church in Philadelphia write: These are the words of the holy one, the true one, who has the key of David, who opens and no one will shut, who shuts and no one opens: "I know your works. Look, I have set before you an open door, which no one is able to shut. I know that you have but little power, and yet you have kept my word and have not denied my name. I will make those of the synagogue of Satan who say that they are Jews and are not, but are lying—I will make them come and bow down before your feet, and they will learn that I have loved you. Because you have kept my word of patient endurance, I will keep you from the hour of trial that is coming on the whole world to test the inhabitants of the earth. I am coming soon; hold fast to what you have, so that no one may seize your crown. If you conquer, I will make you a pillar in the temple of my God; you will never go out of it. I will write on you the name of my God, and the name of the city of my God, the new Jerusalem that comes down from my God out of heaven, and my own new name. Let anyone who has an ear listen to what the Spirit is saying to the churches.

FAITH IN THE CITY

CONTEXT

Philadelphia was founded in the third century BCE with the intention that it be a missionary outpost for Greek language and culture. Now the Christian community is commended for its missionary efforts in the service of a greater cause. Along with Sardis and other area cities it was largely demolished in an earthquake in 17 CE. The resulting aftershocks continued for some time and it was Tiberius Caesar (42 BCE–37 CE) who helped rebuild it.

CHURCH

The congregation may be small, but it has been faithful against the odds. It is the only one of the seven churches against which the Spirit has no complaints. Its members have truly lived by the power of the Christ to open and close doors that appear immovable to human resources. It too is dealing to a certain extent with the outpouring of Christian-Jewish antipathy, and yet is holding firm. It would appear that, despite their physical weakness, a new task is being laid before them, the task of being a pillar in the truly spiritual temple that is being erected. The Spirit will open a door that confronts them in their weakness.

OBSERVATIONS

There are numerous sub/urban congregations in the position of the Philadelphian church. They are faithful and steadfast, not powerful enough to set the world on fire but giving a continuing witness to the Spirit that called them into being. This letter reminds us that God counts importance and worth in a fashion quite different from the world. It also recalls the dependence of the church—of any size—on God. In this case, the participants in the church may have become aware of a need they would like to address. They might actually be able to accomplish this but there is a hurdle before them, a door they cannot open on their own. But as they wait and prepare prayerfully and faithfully, in God's good time, the door is opened. The matter is not so much one of strength, but of spiritual power.

The letter to the Philadelphian Christians invites the members of the sub/urban church to look at the gifts given by the Spirit. Rather than being overwhelmed by what seems impossible, the place to begin is with what is possible. What gifts, skills, connections—even driving questions—do members of the congregation have and what problems can these be brought to address?[22] All of this is in a context where holding to faith is apparently much more difficult and much less rewarding than it once was.

Study 7

Name: Laodicea

Text: Revelation 3:14–22

> And to the angel of the church in Laodicea write: The words of the Amen, the faithful and true witness, the origin of God's creation: "I know your works; you are neither cold nor hot. I wish that you were either cold or hot. So, because you are lukewarm, and neither cold nor hot, I am about to spit you out of my mouth. For you say, 'I am rich, I have prospered, and I need nothing.' You do not realize that you are wretched, pitiable, poor, blind, and naked. Therefore I counsel you to buy from me gold refined by fire so that you may be rich; and white robes to clothe you and to keep the shame of your nakedness from being seen; and salve to anoint your eyes so that you may see. I reprove and discipline those whom I love. Be earnest, therefore, and repent. Listen! I am standing at the door, knocking; if you hear my voice and open the door, I will come in to you and eat with you, and you with me. To the one who conquers I will give a place with me on my throne, just as I myself conquered and sat

---

22. This technique is known as asset-mapping and can be explored through a number of books and web sites.

down with my Father on his throne. Let anyone who has an ear listen to what the Spirit is saying to the churches.

Context

Laodicea was the wealthiest of the seven cities—indeed it was one of the wealthiest in the entire empire. It was established in the third century BCE. When it was destroyed by an earthquake in 61 CE, the residents rebuilt it entirely from private and public monies, declining any help from Rome. It was at the intersection of three major roads and developed its wealth from the garment industry (specializing in raising black sheep), banking and gold exchange, and as a medical center specializing in ophthalmology (primarily ointments and salves). One contextual reality may play into the language of the letter: the community had no local water supply but brought it in from a hot spring via aqueduct. As a result, after the six-mile trip, the water was neither cold nor hot.

Church

This is the only church of the seven about which Christ has nothing good to say. His essential response is: "You are nauseating: tepid, without conviction, and indifferent." Cleverly playing on the Laodiceans' opinions of themselves, the writer notes the categories of their spiritual blindness. Their rich garments and gold are not their true guise but rather mask their lack of integrity and insight. Laodicea, skilled in addressing the physically blind, is spiritually sightless.

Exploring that a little more we can note two problems. First, they were lukewarm in their dedication. Scholars differ as to whether that was at the level of loyalty or at the point of expressing those commitments in action: regardless, they didn't do anything to demonstrate a living faith. Secondly, their self-image was inaccurate; they saw themselves as something they were not: there is a world of difference between "you say" and "you are." It may well be that attending this congregation would be quite pleasant. It certainly wouldn't be challenging, and participants were unlikely to encounter any correction or exhortation. It was smug. It was self-sufficient. It was complacent. They had plenty of money. Perhaps they had beautiful buildings, gifted preachers, a great choir, a great organ, and the respect of the community. They thought they were doing well. What made people comfortable apparently made Jesus ill.

The advice to "buy from me" is an invitation to refocus on the basics or essentials of faith and not to become lost in the minutiae of expression. Gold refined in fire is a common new testament metaphor for a tested and true faith. First, Church Laodicea needed to recover its faith in God. The "white robes" are the apparel of those who have developed an open and honest relationship with the risen Christ. This can be understood in both individual and corporate terms. One of the roles of the Spirit throughout scripture is to open the eyes—physical and spiritual—so that the truth can be seen. The eye ointment (for which Laodicea were noted) is paralleled by a spiritual balm.

This church may have been nauseating to the Spirit, but it was not entirely beyond hope. It is from this reading that one of the most enduring images of Christ's appeal arises. There are countless pictures and stained-glass windows, showing the risen one knocking at the door. If we look closely, the door is generally without a handle. The only way this guest will enter is if those inside open up to the visit. That possibility remains for the church of Laodicea.

Observations

Accurate self-perception is crucial to the success of the sub/urban congregation. One of the reasons for the cognitive dissonance in congregations is that they have not reconsidered themselves and their context for many years. Both have changed, but the members (even if they noticed individual differences) have not come to terms with the totality of difference. "We're a neighborhood church," they claim, ignoring the fact that not one person lives close enough to walk to worship. Or they moan, "This neighborhood doesn't have our kind of people in it anymore," without endeavouring to find out who their neighbors actually are. Local denominational officials were constantly remonstrating with our congregation about the lack of a youth group until we pointed out that, in our area of Halifax, the under 19-years-old population had dropped by over 50 percent in the last fifteen years. There are various denominational and private sector sources that can provide a specialized breakdown of census information for your neighborhood. Local public schools and planning offices also have accurate current and projected data. Simply going for a walk—getting out of the car and on foot—may reveal surprising changes that have been overlooked. Do you know who makes up your neighborhood? Perhaps your context is like ours, where the population during the week is significantly different from the weekend, when the office towers are not buzzing with work. Have you a ministry opportunity—perhaps at lunchtime—to those folks? What about the poor, the dispossessed, and the marginalized? What awareness do you have about their realities and the ways you might, by God's grace, respond? Accurate perception—seeing what is truly there in the church and neighborhood—is crucial to the health of the sub/urban congregation.

Many congregations are terrified of controversy. They have not learned that conflict is a condition of any living organism. Somewhere we learned that "good people don't argue or fight." Conflict will always be present—the issue is whether or not we deal with those conflicts in a healthy and faithful manner. Most of us have seen two congregations that dealt with the same controversial topic and may have arrived at the same conclusion. However, one was stronger because of the process, while another was riven by tension and anger (and perhaps saw folks depart with deep wounds). The difference is largely attributable to the manner of handling conflict. The reality is that vital sub/urban ministry will be marked by conflict because it is characterized by choices. Congregations and clergy must learn how to handle conflict in healthy ways.

Perhaps your congregation has reached the Laodicean crisis because of conflict avoidance. Or perhaps no one has communicated the hard truths of the gospel. Without recreating the clerical theocracy of liberal Protestantism of a previous generation or endorsing the modern dogmatism that masquerades under "the clear word of God" from so many self-appointed Christian spokespeople, the church has both the duty and the opportunity to declare the gospel's clarity. In the retreat from dogmatism, have we so surrendered all clarity to the cause of inoffensive interchange that we miss the fact that those who inhabit the postmodern city, while clearly rejecting many of the hoary authority structures of a previous generation, are also desperately seeking a framework for daily living? They will not flee from an honest presentation of the life of faithfulness that leaves the decision, not in the hands of an authority figure, but in the responsible charge of each believer. There is a sad truth to the fact that membership in Rotary or Kiwanis (or any number of civic groups) is more demanding than membership in some urban congregations.

The letter to Laodicea reminds us of the importance of the basics. It is nice to have buildings, great choirs, and beautiful music. These may have been part of your congregation's past or feature in its present. It's good to have mission, outreach and study groups. These are not wrong—but they are not what the church needs. The vital sub/urban church, even while it expands its presence and service in the community, must always keep a close eye on the basics of church life. Jesus invites them to "buy from me" the things they need. Those are the essentials upon which we can build but from which we become unmoored at our peril.

Summary

The letters to the angels of the churches are specifically directed pieces of correspondence. The introduction and conclusion of each letter reveals intimate knowledge of the context. Each epistle resonates with the firm love of God for these groups of the faithful, and none is so far gone as to have no possibilities. It may be that in reading these case studies you have experienced some light shone on your church community. Perhaps it has happened more than once. Each sub/urban congregation has a unique set of challenges and resources, so faithfulness in each situation will be expressed differently. The purpose of a case study is not to provide one right answer, but to open our own reflecting of the broad range of possibilities present in a given situation and then to decide on our own response, based on reflection, prayer, and our community's unique sense of God's call.

These studies reveal the close relationship between the effectiveness of the church and the community in which it dwells. The challenge is to engage the inner identity of their cities. Those churches that were commended assumed a proactive rather than reactive role. It cannot be stressed too highly, however, that faithfulness looked different in each location:

- In Ephesus, there was a need for rekindled love and the practice of those Christian activities that would promote unity and mutual appreciation in Christ.
- In Smyrna, the issue was taking faith with sufficient seriousness to be willing to suffer if that was the result.
- Pergamum needed to exercise the faith to develop its strength and greater vitality in the congregation's relationship to Christ.
- The church in Thyatira needed to reflect on its own popularity and wrestle with the extent to which that arose from soft-pedalling a demanding Christ.
- The Sardis Church needed to wake up from its comfortable routine and seek a more dynamic Christianity.
- The Philadelphians were selling themselves short: they had done wonderfully in faithful service and had the potential for more in the proclamation, practice and living out of the gospel.
- The church in Laodicea had to come to terms with who they really were, that all the fine accoutrements of their

congregation were concealing a deep rot of spiritual indifference and conventionality. Having seen themselves honestly, they would be open to transformation to a vital faith community.

Two Archetypal Cities

We have been exploring actual cities where Christian ministry occurred. There are two cities in scripture which serve archetypal functions, pushing to extremes both virtues and vices in a way never found in reality for the purpose of making certain points. Both Jerusalem and Babylon appear throughout the bible in their designated roles.

Babylon is the archetype of a city fully given to this world. It is introduced in Genesis 11 in humanity's decision to build a tower. The Plain of Shinar is the later site of Babylon and the tower was probably a ziggurat. The city receives final attention in Revelation 16–18 where it is portrayed as the epitome of evil. For instance, in 17:5 we read: ".and on her forehead was written a name, a mystery: 'Babylon the great, mother of whores and of earth's abominations.'" Like the Jerusalem condemned by the prophets, it was bureaucratic, self-serving, and dehumanizing with an economic structure that benefited the privileged and exploited the poor. Babylon serves as a reminder of the union of a politics of oppression and religion that ignores any claim of God and deifies power and wealth.[23]

As an alternative archetype, we have the idealized Jerusalem that is presented as what a city ought to be (Genesis 14:17–24). It is characterized by the witness of God's shalom (Psalm 122:6–9) by equitable stewardship and by a peaceable and just politics (Exodus 25–40; 1 Samuel 8:4, 20). It is important to balance the archetypal and eschatological portrayal of Jerusalem with its historic reality. However, this archetypal city stood in the place of all cities. Every

---

23. See also Isaiah 14:5–21; Jeremiah 50:2–17; 51:6–10; Daniel 3:17; Revelation 17:1–6; 18:2–19, 24.

first-century Jew believed Jerusalem was the vortex and focus of humanity's spirituality. Therefore, to die in Jerusalem was to die at the spiritual center of the universe.[24] That was why Jesus had to go to Jerusalem to die.[25]

For Reflection and Discussion

- Reread the biblical passages quoted in this chapter. Look for references to the city. What relevance do they have to your own context?
- Using the model in this chapter, try a case study on your faith community. What did you learn?

FAITH IN THE CITY

4.2 GATHERING IN THE CITY

Creating God,
we give you thanks for this quilt we call the city,
with its many coloured and textured squares;
some with bright reds and greens and blues and fine fabric,
shining towers rising from the prosperous pavement,

---

24. Lithicum, *City of God*, 115.
25. Luke 13:34-35 (paralleled by Matthew 23:37-39): "Jerusalem, Jerusalem, the city that kills the prophets and stones those who are sent to it! How often have I desired to gather your children together as a hen gathers her brood under her wings, and you were not willing! See, your house is left to you. And I tell you, you will not see me until the time comes when you say, 'Blessed is the one who comes in the name of the Lord.'" Luke 19:41-44: As he came near and saw the city, he wept over it, saying, "If you, even you, had only recognized on this day the things that make for peace! But now they are hidden from your eyes. Indeed, the days will come upon you, when your enemies will set up ramparts around you and surround you, and hem you in on every side. They will crush you to the ground, you and your children within you, and they will not leave within you one stone upon another; because you did not recognize the time of your visitation from God."

stately houses residing on quiet streets
fringed by the shade of welcoming trees,
others not so bright, worn thin by worry and stress,
colours washed out to grey and beige and black
by violence and hunger,
tangled threads edging lives unloved
in hostels and shelters open to the winds of indifference and poverty.
But we know that you, O God, are the Maker of our quilt
and you wish nothing more than for your people
to live in prosperity and peace,
finding shelter
in your many-coloured
coverings of love.
Thank you
May it be so. [26]

The sub/urban church *does* many things. In fact, that's one of the joys and challenges of that form of spiritual community: there is often a constant buzz of activity. If communities of faith take seriously the invitation in these pages to work cooperatively with other groups, the level of activity might actually increase. Imagine a church building used seven days a week, not simply for the internal programs of the congregation but by a host of differing groups striving to nurture health, healing, and community in the midst of the crushing anonymity of metropolitan life. The challenge—nay the danger—is that we can become absorbed in the management of this teeming life and forget the purpose for which this well-used structure was originally erected and lovingly maintained: the worship of God. It is in worship that our words and metaphors about the Christian journey come together and it is there that we determine whether or not the experience will be some form of retreat from sub/urban life or a hallowing and challenging of it. Jeremiah calls on us to "seek the welfare of the city" (29:7), perhaps in response to attitudes of people who didn't really want to be there.

26. Hardy, *Worship in the City*, 58.

God's folks have a calling to care for their neighbors in that great soup of differing humanity which is the city.[27]

Ideally, the church is the place where often very diverse people gather in ways that they might not otherwise encounter one another. In truth, too many congregations reproduce the divisions of the city around them. But, at least the church holds to the ideal of unity in Christ in the diversity of humanity and should both confess its homogeneity and seek to overcome it. We gather to invoke God's presence in the sub/urban environment—not because God needs our invitation but to declare to ourselves, and anyone who will attend, that the city is not beyond the care of the divine and that the reign of God is found here as much as anywhere. The church, made up of people who do not agree on everything, can model for the city the ways of living with conflict and difference, confession and forgiveness, inclusion and vision. Without that creative spiritual vision, the city will wither and die.

So, we need good symbols, singable tunes, and credible words that extol our gratitude for the hand of the divine in both the built and natural environments. My congregation loves to sing "We Plough the Fields and Scatter."[28] But we don't *do* that. At best, folks have small backyard gardens or a small plot in the growing number of shared community gardens appearing in many cities. Similarly, we don't "Bring in the Sheaves,"[29] yet every Thanksgiving there are wheat sheaves and corn stalks as well as different types of produce—mostly purchased at a grocery store—decorating the sanctuary. To be fair, in recent years we have seen increasing numbers of canned goods *and* all the food (regardless of the form) goes immediately to the local food pantry. But the music and the symbolism harkens back to a form and place of living which is not only foreign to the current lived experience of the worshippers but, for

27. There is a growing number of resources for sub/urban worship in recent years. Many of those are, however, not gathered in one place, but scattered across the Internet on the sites of those congregations that make their services available. One resource is Hardy, *Worship in the City*. See also the *Voices United* and *More Voices* hymn resources (1996, 2007).

28. Author: Matthias Claudius (1782); translated by Jane M. Campbell.

29. Words: Knowles Shaw (1874); tune: George A. Minor (1880).

most of them, *has never been their setting.* These are sub/urban people, born and bred, and yet when the time for Thanksgiving comes they, without any reflection, decorate their sacred space with objects foreign to their experience. How can that not create a disconnect?

Similarly, during Advent, the church school pageant coincides with the gathering of white and pink gifts.[30] Every year there is the challenge of psycho-spiritually moving worshippers from a rural setting (the natural association of mangers and animals) to a crowded sub/urban center which is somewhat better aligned to a crowded Bethlehem. And, every year that a sub/urban contextual reality is introduced—through drama, prayers, symbols, and so on—I know I will receive complaints from someone that we have "ruined Christmas" for them. In that case, Christmas as a "Hallmark moment" seems to function both as an honoring of some vague childish memory and, as a way of keeping the realistic demands of incarnation from disrupting our tidy lives. Again, worship has been relegated to some "special place" in which worshippers retreat as break from the demanding sub/urban life to which they will return all-too-soon.

Saying and singing words that are relevant are an important part of Protestant worship.[31] The joys and sorrows, the heartbreak and ecstasy of a week in God's world are the substance of our faithfulness. Just as we want to feel at home in our places of residence, so we want to feel at home in our place of worship. There are those in sub/urban life who feel a real sense of displacement. For those folks feeling at home in worship—at home in the city in worship—it can be psychologically and spiritually crucial in their disorientation.

---

30. White gifts—age appropriate toys and clothes—are used for Christmas hampers; pink gifts—toiletries, etc.—are given to local shelters for women and children.

31. It might be argued in some traditions that connecting with historic language used for centuries is the core of liturgy. I choose to sidestep a debate in which I am not equipped to engage.

Prayer

When the community prays, we gather together our sense of God in our lives. We can bring all things to God for God already knows all things and continues to love us. We bring the experiences of life to consciousness and articulation, not because God needs to hear them but because, in so doing, we become conscious of the presence of the Spirit nourishing, nurturing, and healing our lives and the life of creation. Whether your tradition is of communal prayer, or of prayers offered by a worship leader for the sake of the wider community, it is important that the words not only gather up a range of experience but speak in a language and metaphor the worshippers can own. Obviously, much prayer is neither rural, small town, nor sub/urban specific:

> Holy God, gentle guide, bless us as we gather here with the comfort and challenge of your presence. Quiet our fears, renew our courage, open our eyes to see you in those around us, and inspire in us the desire to speak and act for justice and peace in our homes, in our communities, and in our world. So, may we be your people, wide in mercy and deep in love. In Jesus' name, we pray, Amen.

However, if we were to move into thanksgiving, it would be appropriate to raise for appreciation a multitude of differing causes. Thus, the prayer leader should consider the various ways in which the city is a source of blessing: the people and activities that keep the city safe and moving, the place of arts, athletics, cultural festivals, and so on. As an example, many sub/urban congregations are incorporating a "Blessing of Bicycles," catching up both on a particularly sub/urban form of transportation (as opposed to entertainment or exercise), and the conflict that arises between vehicles and bicycles. For instance:

> Present in a world groaning under the excesses of consumption we acknowledge the inherent goodness of non-motorized human powered transportation and give thanks for the simple beauty of the bicycle. God of life, Hear our prayer.

Present in a community filled with children we pray for those learning to ride. Keep them smart, safe and visible on their neighborhood roads. God of life, Hear our prayer.

Present in a community filled with strife we pray for the victims of road rage, and bike theft. And we ask for the strength to forgive mean people, and to be set free from the prisons of our own anger. God of life, Hear our prayer.

Present in a world of work we pray for those who build, repair and clean our bikes and those who rely on bicycles to earn their living. Bless those who choose to not drive to work and those for whom driving isn't even an option. God of life, Hear our prayer.

Present in a community of beautiful diversity we ask your protection and blessing on all who ride; Pedi cabbies, weekend warriors, athletes, homeless folks, students, children, eco-warriors, bike co-op anarchists, messengers and all the others who take to the streets, bike paths, parks and mountains of our communities. Keep us safe as we ride. God of life, Hear our prayer.

We now observe a moment of silence for all who have died while riding.

God of life, Hear our prayer. AMEN[32]

When we turn to confession we can also lift up items which may not be sub/urban specific, yet certainly resonate. Obviously, anxiety and misgiving, fear and distrust, ignoring of the cries of the needy, and reluctance to follow Christ are universal spiritual realities with which we struggle. However, what if we were to confess our fear and distrust of "the neighbour who speaks another language and the newcomer who follows a different faith and the

---

32. See http://www.chesapeakespokes.org/library/Bike_Blessing_2014.pdf adapting a liturgy from *A House for All Sinners and Saints* (Denver, CO).

fellow-passenger on the bus who is clothed in strange-looking garments"? Can we make our ignoring more specific to the "hands that reach out to us on the street and the well-meaning folk urging us to sign their petitions as we brush by hurrying to our next appointment"? What about the Christ we ignore in "the person sleeping in the bus shelter, preaching in front of the public garden, huddling outside the hospital while desperately smoking, the breakfast program feeding kids who don't get enough at home"?

Confession also allows us to employ the little-used pattern of lament.[33] One of the important advantages of the lament, particularly in response to the individualism of the city, is that it allows us to express anger and dismay at injustice and oppression for which we are not the direct cause. Often people will find themselves blocked in an appropriate response to tragedy or cruelty because our default response to wrong is guilt. But if we can legitimately declare, "I didn't do it," worshippers may feel stuck in how to respond (for instance, to examples of systemic societal racism when they are not, in practice, racist). Lament allows us to mourn, in company with the creator of all, and seek the hope of healing and restoration. It also avoids another common sub/urban failing: the sense that we have to do it all and every social concern is simply one more burden to carry. Lament allows us to trust God while at the same time declaring, "It's just not right!"

When we think of intercession, prayer writers are encouraged to be specific about the pains of the neighborhood and city, recognizing the wholeness and restoration that are needed around the block as well as around the world. It is a wonderful opportunity to catch up on events that might be in the local media as well as the conversations in the coffee shop. As well as concern for nature we can pray for the built environment—both the beautiful and the ugly. It is always appropriate to lift up the many forms of violence that lurk around the corner in the city.

---

33. Bartlett, *Lamentations for Lent: Whom Shall I Fear: Lenten Reflections on the Psalms of Lament.*

Symbols

Much of worship—some may argue too much—is centered around words. We sing, pray, read, preach, and converse in words. Some part of worship involves action. We stand, sit, and kneel; we break bread, pour water, lay on hands, dance, proclaim God in drama. We gather in places that are replete with symbols. Even the simplest and most austere meeting house, in its very sparseness, gives us symbols of intent: a bible (open or closed); candle(s); a cross (with a figure or empty, large and dominating, or barely visible); a basin and towel; a font (large and prominent, or small and tucked away until occasionally employed); stained glass windows and banners. All of those symbols proclaim something to the worshiper about the commitments of this gathered community. My experience suggests that we are not always as attentive to these as we might be. Indeed, some of them may have been gathered over decades and actually conflict with one another. Sometimes, we simply have to live with what we have inherited because the costs involved in removal (either monetary or in terms of conflict) are greater than the reward. But, where we can exercise some control, what symbols might we employ that speak more clearly to the sub/urban context of our worship? Symbols and actions appropriately added to worship will enhance the impact of the service, not merely for the non-literate, pre-literate, and too distracted to concentrate. I suggest that, if there are creative and artistic people in your congregation—and I have never known one without them (even if they are sometimes marginalized)—you employ their special gifts. Here are some starting places:

Table 3: Biblical Images and Contemporary Parallels

If the Bible speaks of	Sub/urban images (in actual or photo form)
Desert	A snow swept mall parking lot
	A multi lane intersection at rush hour
	A downtown business street on Sunday morning
	A car wrecking site

Thanksgiving for produce	The tools people in your congregation use to make a living—computers, industrial machines, etc.
	Varieties of bread—also for World Communion—reflecting different ethnicities in your community
	Soccer or football
	Concert or theatre ticket
Walking a path	Via Dolorosa from Jerusalem
	Walkway in a park
	Barbed wire
	Keep out signs
	Beware of Dog
Temptation	Empty liquor bottle
	Lottery ticket
	Big box store
	Glittering ads
Easter	Different colored fabrics
	A potted plant
	A Habitat for Humanity build
	A Help Wanted or Now Hiring sign
	Group cleaning up a highway
	City park
Maundy Thursday	Bowl and towel
	Picture of a waiter
	Picture of city worker
	Folks gathered in a diner

Summer	Picture of fountain or splash pad
	Take worship outside
	Concerts in the park
	Ice cream truck
Pentecost	Different street signs that catch up different nationalities
	Different places of worship
	Crowd scenes
Christmas	Downtown shelter
	Crowd at airport or train station
	Have the pageant birth Emmanuel is a place consistent with your context
General	Look for images/pictures that catch up Matthew 25
	Mix natural symbols with built environment—e.g., trees with bricks or shingles
	Candles
	Pray through the neighborhood with stops at different places—often appropriate for Good Friday (liturgies can be found online)

Music

For Protestants especially, singing is a primary vehicle for the sharing and remembering theology. Finding hymns that are redolent with sub/urban images is both challenging and increasingly rewarding. It is a challenge to find hymns in traditional hymnbooks (even recent publications) that celebrate the positive aspects of the city. On the other hand, with the Internet there is a growing (albeit still small) trove of city-positive hymns. So, my encouragement to you is to scour the resources you have available to find hymns and songs that reflect the reality of the city and go beyond poverty and pollution. Most hymnbooks have indices of topics and words. Some even publish a computer-searchable version. Recall some of the concepts we've explored in this study: community life, worship, diversity, seeking, lament, God's call, comfort, and healing. Another possibility is the use of world and global music which help the worshipping community contact the folks who come to the city from many different places.[34]

For Reflection and Discussion

- Consider each aspect of church life discussed in this chapter. Can you think of your favorite example? Can you think of examples that might be more contextually appropriate for your faith community?
- Study the worship resources used in your community (hymn books, slides, prayer books, service books, etc.) Look for resources that speak specifically to the sub/urban context. What gaps or surprises do you find?

---

34. See the list from *Voices United* and *More Voices* found in Hardy, *Worship in the City*, 18–21. Some of those hymns appear in other denominational resources.

Chapter 5

Speaking Church

A New Vision for the Sub/Urban Congregation

> Maker—Spirit—Son, God of grace and love,
> we call you by many names—Elohim, Yahweh, Seigneur, Creator,
> and feel ourselves named by you—
> forgetful, forgiven, beloved.
> We gather in this place to pray and praise
> and consider the way we name ourselves and others...
> Help us to be open to your Word and your World. Amen[1]

BECAUSE THE CITY HAS such an overwhelming physical presence, it is easy to forget that it owes everything—origin, existence, renovation, and personality—to human speech. Words are everywhere. They are used by ordinary citizens, media, advertisers, a myriad of officials and politicians, and on and on. The irony is that language is often seen as ineffectual. We are told to "walk the walk" rather than "talk the talk" as if the former makes the world and the latter merely comments. And yet, for people of the book (Moslem, Jewish and Christian), words are constitutive of reality. God speaks, and things become: "Let there be light, and there was light." But

---

1. Hardy, *Worship in the City*, 131.

every building began in speech, one way or another. It is so easy to forget, especially with block upon block of buildings in the metropolis. We may forget that the bodies—the human beings who populate this concrete jungle—are beings that speak, and their communicating is what creates and sustains the city life.²

As we have seen, because of the mixtures of types and motivations in the city, some have despaired of sub/urban life. To quote a respected observer of North American religious life:

> In a world where strangers meet strangers with gunfire, barrier walls, spiritually land-mined paths, the spirit of revenge, and the record of intransigence, it sounds almost dainty to come on the scene and urge that hospitality has a strong and promising place.³

And yet, that is what happens in the city. There, people of all circumstances, wealthy and impoverished, strong and feeble, talented and ordinary, well-and evil-intended meet and interact. None is entirely sure how they manage to do that without massive destruction of people and place. Expressions of disapproval abound. Frustration and resentment build up and boil over. Graffiti and demonstrations make points that are ignored in polite speech and letters to the editor.

All of this is framed by and empowered in words. If a city is a great place to live because of its many amenities and services, it is primarily so because the majority of conversation occurs responsibly, civilly, and with some attention to components of truth, dignity, appropriateness, and consequence. Thus, of all the sounds we can apprehend in the city, the human voice is the most exceptional in quantity and range of tone, texture, and content.

Urbanization is the great human reality of our time. It varies from country to country, of course. In Canada, for instance, fully 53 percent of the nation's gross domestic product (GDP) is generated by five metropolitan regions. This is significantly more than, for instance, the United States where the five largest cities generate

---

2. Yi-Fu Tuan, "The City," 144–151.
3. Marty, *When Faiths Collide*, 128.

only 23 percent of GDP. More than 80 percent of Canadians are piled into 2 percent of the land mass, making it much more urban than its southern neighbor and even parts of Europe.[4] Thus, for a Canadian pastor and theologian, these are quite pressing realities. However, our cities (while generally lacking the shocking violent crime statistics associated with their American counterparts) are rapidly shifting. A study conducted of Toronto in 2010 showed that while in 1970 two-thirds of the city reported an average middle income (plus/minus 10 percent), by 2000 that number had shrunk to one-third. Instead of one city, that creates three rings: an immensely wealthy core where only a very few can afford to live; an extreme periphery of disconnection, disadvantage, and poverty; and, a middle ring of shrinking middle-and working-class families.[5] Thus, rather than urban core, the growing locus for urban mission is the suburb.

So, what is the city as a locus for Christian ministry? What would a vision for a faithful sub/urban congregation look like?

a. Contextual: For the local church, the purpose of theology is an aid to hearing and living the good news for the sake of the place where God has called us into existence. That has several impacts. Faithful sub/urban Christians must constantly be translating. We are disciples (students) of Jesus Christ and no one has ever been us in this place at this time. Therefore, we must look with critical faithfulness at all received models, testing them for the eternal truths applicable in our context. In a church that is often anxious about numbers (revenue, attendance, etc.), this is a particularly relevant warning about the next great plan to increase those. In my studies, I have seen communities of faith that are thriving with every imaginable form of liturgy (and some I never imagined) because they did the work of faithfully discerning the Spirit's call to

---

4. Florida, *Who's Your City?*, xii, 10.

5. David Hulchanski, " Three Cities Within Toronto: Income Polarization," a report, 2010. http://www.urbancentre.utoronto.ca/pdfs/curp/tnrn/Three-Cities-Within-Toronto-2010-Final.pdf Accessed April 8, 2016.

them. And it is different from the call to the church down the street which in also thriving in a different style.

b. Communal: The city gives an impression of anonymity. The suburbs, which are often so dependent on the personal vehicle, appear to exacerbate that aloneness. Sub/urban life can often be divisive of the individual, requiring people to go to many different places to have various professional and service needs met. However, if it is sufficiently nimble, the church is ideally positioned to respond to another, equally powerful, force in sub/urban life. Wherever one goes, we see groups of people gathering. These are not the patterns of institutional affiliation of a generation ago. Indeed, historic service clubs, fraternal organizations, and organized sports groups often struggle with the same numerical realities facing churches. However, these newer groups are based on shared interests which often transcend social, cultural, economic, racial, and religious boundaries. In this sub/urban re-clustering, the church is well-positioned to play a positive role because we are, by our most basic mandate, concerned with the whole person—and particularly the stranger. If people inside and outside the church today have an apathetic view of organized religion, it may be because we have been better at building walls than employing ancient paths of life-transformation.

c. Contextually aware: In order to undertake faithful sub/urban ministry we must know about our context. Do you know who lives in a five-mile radius of your church building? Who are they? Do they own or rent; what's the second most common language spoken; what are the levels of formal education: what are the principal employers; how many receive various forms of assistance? What are the real issues facing the community?

d. Cooperative: If the gospel is "good news for the poor" as Jesus announced, one of the realities for sub/urban churches is that many of the challenges to fullness of life in our communities is that they are beyond the resources we can deploy alone.

So, faithful sub/urban churches must learn how to move into partnerships with other organizations. For some this will be harder than for others, because community groups may not be faith-based—or may indeed be based in other faiths or traditions. We may have to learn what is essential and what is peripheral to our call at this moment. For instance, how important is the faith basis for our actions if we work with the local mosque to clean up and make safe a park where all our children play? To learn about our own mission field (the one right outside our front doors), it is crucial to be in conversation and cooperation with other organizations and groups. One of the things that a sub/urban church (which may feel acutely its lack of numbers) brings to the table is often space that can be used for meetings, programs, and the like.

e. Open and outward: If you consider the expenditures—time and money—of your local congregation, how many of them are directed inward and how many outward? The sad reality is that, for many churches, the overwhelming percentage of resources are directed inward: maintaining a comfortable ritual, a welcoming fellowship, and pastoral care for insiders. That's what is expected of clergy in a rarely questioned worldview which says that's their job. That is a holdover from a previous worldview which persisted for 1,500 years, wherein the job of the folks in the pews was to provide the resources (primarily financial) so that experts—missionaries, overseas personnel, theologians, and local clergy—could do ministry for them. With the change in context (noted above), all of that has been invalidated, but word hasn't yet gotten through and those most responsible for conveying it—local pastors—have been unwilling or unable to do so. Our scriptural tradition repeatedly speaks of God giving various gifts for the ministry of the body. So, why has Christ appointed some people in every church to function in these capacities? Paul responds, "[Christ did this] to prepare God's people for works of service." (Eph 4:12) This is the single most important principle for effective urban ministry. What that passage tells us is that *the urban church is not meant to be a shelter; it is meant to be a seminary.*

If sub/urban churches are to survive and, more importantly, play a faithful role as the Spirit calls them, that ratio of resources will need to change. We, all of us, will need to recognize that the call of Christ is right outside the door. For centuries, it was common for Christians to speak of the "mission field" as being someplace far away where we took something we had (the gospel) to them because they needed it. The language of "mission field" doesn't work for the contemporary sub/urban church because we don't need to transport God from one place to another; we need to recognize where God already is. As communities of faith, we hold a tradition that maintains that God is everywhere, and our special *charism* is seeing that presence and pointing it out.[6] Our search is for life. For, "[W]here Jesus is, there is life. There is abundant life, vigorous life, loved life, and eternal life. There is life before death."[7] As he goes on to observe, in terms that are particularly applicable to the sub/urban setting, we have often come to accept death as normal: death through violence, racism, labelling of the other, death on the streets and in the boardroom, and the death of human hope. As the disciples of the one who has shown that life is greater than death, we are needed in the city.

f. Metaphor and story rather than argument: The city is often the home for the post-modern person. Sometimes people of faith mistake these folks as self-absorbed, flighty, and undisciplined—the "spiritual but not religious" crowd. True, some are. But many are deeply committed to a search for a meaningful spiritual life. They just don't see the traditional church as a resource in that journey. However, if what I have said previously about metaphor and story is true than the church

---

6. Of course, that may raise significant faith development issues if we have no experience in doing that outside the comfortable confines we call "religious." Bell, *Velvet Elvis*, 96.

7. Moltmann, *The Passion for Life*, 22.

is in a wonderful place to connect with such folks—assuming we can set aside the proposition and argument styles that served in the modern era. The general characteristics of your post-modern neighbor include: a preference for story over argument; a hunger for affiliation and belonging; curiosity about and openness to genuine life in community; being convinced that truth is relational rather than propositional; a tolerant of diversity; and an expectation of a smorgasbord or buffet of choices rather than a one-size-fits all approach. So, the challenge to the sub/urban church is to shape the faith story so that our neighbors can hear it. Before you get all up in arms, remember that we followed one who preferred to tell a story rather than argue the law, and spoke of such outrageous notions as a *good* Samaritan. He spoke of the kingdom of God, something that was "in the midst of you" or "within your grasp."[8] Can we be as creative?

Post-modern is not necessarily a matter of age as it is one of experience and outlook. Most of us are so bombarded with advertising and political messages and various causes shouting for our attention that we have become, as a matter of self-preservation, cynical and skeptical. Anyone aged fifty or over has lived through the apparent failure of science and technology to solve all of society's problems. When we are told that something is "bigger," "faster," or "better," we are doubtful. If your conversation partner is a post-modern, that is all to your advantage. For post-moderns, anything presented with a four-step program and diagrams is immediately suspect because they feel intuitively that the truth comes in far less packaged ways. It comes as poetry and art. It is a story and discovered in the interaction of people. It comes less as "something I have that you need to have too," than as "this is how I see the world, what do you see?" So, we are less likely to offend the other person if we are not claiming

---

8. Luke 17:20. The Greek phrase is *entos humon,* which has sometimes been mistakenly translated to "within you," encouraging a concentration on the individual spiritual life, and a split between the inner and outer person.

to have something they need, but merely sharing the wonder of our common pilgrimage in life. Like you, I have had the experience of someone telling me why I needed to have exactly what they had—and were often trying to sell me. It's boring, tiresome, and sometimes offensive. I have never, ever been offended when someone told me that something was important to them and why. I may not have felt the need for whatever it was in my life, but I wasn't offended by hearing their story.

One final note about metaphor. In our society, there is a "proper meaning superstition" which holds that a word has a meaning of its own (preferably only one) that applies in all situations. However, language is malleable in time and culture.[9] When we draw some of our root language from texts that are all more than 1,900 years old, we need to be constantly aware of that. Though I love modern English translations of the bible, there is the regular risk of assuming that recognizing a word implies knowing its meaning in context. Stability in meaning should never be assumed.

Metaphors call forth feelings and attitudes. They influence both perception and interpretation.[10] That's one reason why powerful metaphors can also be highly controversial. For example, the metaphor of God as father draws on a constellation of associations: positive, negative, and neutral, depending on both the context and the listener. But for a speaker who has surrendered to the "proper meaning superstition," this is no longer a metaphor; denial of the "fatherhood of God" may be received as dismissing a "fact" as real as gravity. Rudolph Bultmann insisted that our society has an epidemic of reading everything literally.[11] God as father is, for many, a dead metaphor: it has entered the language game and one component has been entirely absorbed by the other. Other examples

---

9. Zwicky, *Wisdom*, 11.
10. Barbour, *Myths, Models and Paradigms*, 47.
11. Stonehouse, et al., *Parable, Myth and Language*, 58.

of dead metaphors include, "the arm of the chair," "the eye's lid," "handing over," or "handing down" information.

In a rural church in Mexico I saw a visual representation of a dead metaphor. It was a towering statue of an old, white man, with long white hair and grey robe, seated on a throne. On the knees, in much smaller proportions, were a bleeding figure on a cross and a small white bird. Enough said.

g. Displacement: Earlier I offered "displacement" as a metaphor to help us understand the setting of the sub/urban church. Employed here, it implies that we have remained in the same physical location and that most, if not all, of the features of the society around us remain unchanged. We go to familiar places and everything appears the same but are somehow different. The circles of power and influence look much the same in the city, but there's no place reserved for us. Instead, the church or its representatives are trotted out now and again to serve other people's agendas. Many clergy people experience this at weddings and before banquets. It's called displacement. Further, through legislative changes and shifts in immigration, the face of the North American city has been transformed into a multi-cultural and multi-religious society.

Metaphor can be an extremely powerful tool in assisting the urban church in the understanding and articulating of its vision. By making this claim, I am asserting that the way in which God's people perceive and name the world has an impact on what we call "reality." In suggesting new metaphors, we are trying to understand how new insights might be true and empower a new understanding of our lives. The new metaphor may also allow us to fit in aspects of experience which could not be encompassed in more traditional metaphors.[12]

Given the range of literary styles in the bible, it is quite surprising that theological reflection has dominated theology for so long. As Amos Wilder says of the New Testament, "[the] writings are in large part works of the imagination, loaded, charged and

---

12. Lakoff and Johnson, *Metaphors*, 154, 172.

encrusted with every kind of figurative resource and invention."[13] In recent decades, other forms of theology and study have come into greater prominence. However, most Protestant study and proclamation in North America employs reflection as the method to determine the right answer to "what the passage means." As we reflect on "speaking church" in a new era, we must wrestle with whether or not we even want precision in religious language. Will we simply exchange one set of restraints for another? However, in a society obsessed with the "literal," can the church afford the resultant confusion of even more metaphorical speech?

Some Ideas Along the Way—Not Really Conclusions

Why is a contextual theology needed for the sub/urban congregation? Because the sub/urban church is different and needs its own resources for faithful life and mission. There is the regular risk of confusing an idealized rural life with the Christian *koinonia*. We need ways of relating the gospel in a meaningful manner to the urban area. Such a theology must come to terms with the fact that "community" in the city has its own demands. If we employ a law/gospel distinction, the "law" is the driving conformity that the city exercises in so many ways to accept others' choices for us. From the media to the peer group to the local politicians, the city is replete with pressures to accept the idea that what others tell us ought to be important, truly will be so for us. In this context, "gospel" is the summon to make choices and accept the responsibility for those choices. So, some quick signposts of where the vital sub/urban church can and must play a role in the life of the city.

First: Creating communities that welcome and address the whole person, rather than the compartmentalized creature that the city addresses.

Second: Speaking the truth. Talking back to increasingly centralized media control and providing tools to sort out the huge

---

13. Wilder, *The Language of Gospel*, 128.

range of internet possibilities. How can we be wise *and* faithful consumers of news regarding the creation God loves?

Third: Related to my second point, finding a place where the church can speak a gospel response to the already sanitized news that comes to us, allegedly to protect us. An independent, scripturally-ground, life-committed church can respond to the many kinds of false speech.

Fourth: The sub/urban environment presents rich opportunities to engage in collaborative justice-seeking and truth-stating work with other groups. Today's justice seekers come from a range of backgrounds and organizations. The city congregation brings to the conversation a continuity of expression. I dare to suggest that a sub/urban congregation should not engage in any sort of work unless it is collaborative.

Fifth: A sub/urban church that is rooted in its surroundings and in its scriptures will be committed to hearing the voice of God in the cries of the oppressed. A biblically formed people will recognize the unreality of so-called "neutrality." Christians who have read their scriptures know that God is not neutral, for such "objectivity" amounts to a reinforcement of the status quo. The sub/urban church must either undertake or support those who undertake the analysis of the causes of injustice. As it denounces the shortcomings, it can also declare a positive vision of human society as the basis for dreaming the vision of a new city.

> *We are simply asked*
> *to make gentle a bruised world*
> *to tame its savageness;*
> *to be compassionate of all (including oneself);*
> *then in the time left over*
> *to repeat the ancient tale*
> *and go the way*
> *of God's foolish ones.* (written by an anonymous Jesuit)

As I walked the streets of New York City on Good Friday, I was struck by the thought—is this what it was like in Jerusalem so long ago? In any other place I've been, Good Friday is a statutory holiday and the atmosphere is radically different—especially downtown. In New York that day, it was just like any other. Manhattan's sidewalks were crammed with people, the sounds of a dozen different languages and dialects falling on my ears. The streets themselves were filled with fleets of urgent, honking, pressing traffic. There was some sort of security alert that led to a noticeable increase in armed soldiers at the intersections (perhaps like Jerusalem on that tense Passover weekend.) All of these folks were going about their lives, living out their story and—in different places here and there—some of those who called themselves Jesus-Followers were gathering to remember. In Little Italy, we stumbled across the end of a community Stations of the Cross parade, with a couple of hundred parishioners from two or three parishes following a group of costumed folks to the "tomb" in the middle of an elementary school play yard. Police (off-duty? on overtime? supplied by the city?) were providing traffic control as these folks told a portion of their faith story in word and song and the narrative of an ancient, cruel, and ever-relevant event. I overheard a young mother trying to explain to her daughter what it was all about, this story being played out which was, apparently, just on the edge of her knowledge.

For Reflection and Discussion

- Consider the five "signposts" of a vital and faithful sub/urban church as listed in this chapter. Which one(s) characterize your faith community? Describe that. How might you move forward on the others?

Bibliography

Barbour, Ian G. *Myths, Models and Paradigms: A Comparative Study in Science and Religion.* New York: Harper and Row, 1976.

Bartlett, Ross. *Lamentations for Lent: Whom Shall I Fear: Lenten Reflections on the Psalms of Lament.* Toronto: United Church Publishing House, 2004.

Bell, Rob. *Velvet Elvis: Repainting the Christian Faith.* New York: HarperCollins, 2012.

Berger, Peter, ed. *The Desecularization of the World: Resurgent Religion and World Politics.* Grand Rapids: Eerdmans, 1999.

Bevans, Stephen B. *Models of Contextual Theology.* Maryknoll, NY: Orbis, 1992.

Bibby, Reginald. *Restless Gods: The Renaissance of Religion in Canada.* Toronto: Stoddart, 2002.

Brown, Robert Macafee. *Theology in a New Key: Responding to Liberation Themes.* Philadelphia: Westminster, 1978.

Conn, Harvie M. *A Clarified Vision for Urban Mission: Dispelling the Urban Stereotypes.* Grand Rapids: Zondervan, 1987.

Cox, Harvey. "The Myth of the Twentieth Century: The Rise and Fall of 'Secularization.'" In *The Twentieth Century: A Theological Overview,* edited by Gregory Baum, 135–43. Maryknoll, NY: Orbis, 1999.

———. *Fire from Heaven: The Rise of Pentecostal Spirituality and the Reshaping of Religion in the 21st Century.* Reading, MA: Perseus Books, 1995.

Florida, Richard. *Who's Your City?* Toronto: Vintage Canada, 2009.

Gomez, Liliana and Walter Van Herck, eds. *The Sacred in the City.* London: Bloomsbury, 2013.

Gornik, Mark. *To Live in Peace: Biblical Faith and the Changing Inner City.* Grand Rapids: Eerdmans, 2003.

Gorringe, T.J. *A Theology of the Built Environment: Justice, Empowerment, Redemption.* Cambridge: Cambridge University Press, 2002.

Guittierez, Gustavo. *A Theology of Liberation.* Translated by C. Inda and J. Eagleson. Maryknoll, NY: Orbis, 1973.

Hardy, Nancy Elizabeth. *Worship in the City: Prayers and Songs for Urban Settings.* Toronto: United Church Publishing House, 2015.

BIBLIOGRAPHY

Harper, Nile. *Urban Churches, Vital Signs: Beyond Charity Toward Justice.* Grand Rapids: Eerdmans, 1998.

Heifetz, Ronald. *Leadership Without Easy Answers.* Cambridge: Harvard University Press, 1998.

Hobsbawm, Eric J. *The Age of Extremes: A History of the World, 1914–1997.* New York: Vintage Books, 1996.

Jacobs, Jane. *The Death and Life of Great American Cities.* New York: Vintage Books, 1963.

Lakoff, George and Mark Johnson. *Metaphors We Live By,* Chicago: University of Chicago Press, 1980.

Leong, David P. *Street Signs: Toward a Missional Theology of Urban Cultural Engagement.* Eugene, OR: Pickwick, 2012.

Lithicum, Robert C. *City of God, City of Satan: A Biblical Theology of the Urban Church.* Grand Rapids: Zondervan, 1991.

MacCormac, Earl R. *A Cognitive Theory of Metaphor.* Cambridge, MA: MIT Press, 1985.

Marcos, Louis A. "Speaking Out: Poetry-Phobic: Why evangelicals should love language that is slippery." *Christianity Today* (blog), *Christianitytoday.com,* Oct. 1, 2001, http://www.ctlibrary.com/ct/2001/october1/26.66.html.

Marty, Martin. *When Faiths Collide.* Oxford: Blackwell, 2005.

McFague, Sallie. *Speaking in Parables: A Study in Metaphor and Theology.* Philadelphia: Fortress, 1975.

———. *Metaphorical Theology: Models of God in Religious Language.* Philadelphia: Fortress, 1982.

Mead, Loren. *More Than Numbers: The Way That Churches Grow.* Bethesda, MD: Alban, 1993.

Meyers, Eleanor Scott, ed. *Envisioning the New City: A Reader on Urban Ministry.* Louisville: Westminster John Knox, 1992.

Minear, Paul S. *Images of the Church in the New Testament.* Philadelphia: Westminster, 1960.

Moltmann, Jurgen Moltmann. *The Passion for Life,* trans M Douglas Meeks. Philadelphia:Fortress, 1978.

Northcott, Michael, ed. *Urban Theology: A Reader.* London: Cassells, 1998.

Petrie, Hugh G. "Do you see what I see? The epistemology of interdisciplinary inquiry." *Journal of Aesthetic Education* 10 (January 1976) 29–43.

Robinson, Anthony. *Transforming Congregational Culture.* Grand Rapids: Eerdmans, 2003.

Saunders, Stanley P., and Charles L. Campbell. *The Word on the Street: Performing the Scriptures in the Urban Context.* Grand Rapids: Eerdmans, 2000.

Selles, Otto. "Faith in Poetry: Religious language, believing and non-. *Books and Culture,* May 1, 2003, read online (1.16.2007) at https://www.booksandculture.com/articles/2003/mayjun/5.21.html.

Stonehouse, Tony, et al. *Parable, Myth and Language.* Washington DC: College of Preachers, 1967.

BIBLIOGRAPHY

Tuan, Y-Fu. "The City and Human Speech." *Geographical Review* 84 (April 1994) 144–51.

Wilder, Amos. *The Language of the Gospel: Early Christian Rhetoric.* New York: Harper & Row, 1964.

Williams, Dolores S. "Rub Poor Lil' Judas's Head." *The Christian Century* 107 (October 1990) 963.

Wuthnow, Robert. *Christianity in the Twenty-first century: Reflections on the Challenges Ahead.* New York: Oxford University Press, 1993.

Zwicky, Jan. *Wisdom and Metaphor.* Kentville, Canada: Gaspereau, 2003.

www.ingramcontent.com/pod-product-compliance
Lightning Source LLC
Chambersburg PA
CBHW050834160426
43192CB00010B/2021